**A BLUEPR...
YOUR ACTIV...
SUPPORT FOR THE CAUSES YOU
CARE ABOUT, FEATURING
FAN-BUILDING TACTICS FROM
THE MUSIC INDUSTRY AND THE
VOICES OF TODAY'S MOST
PASSIONATE CHANGE-MAKERS**

From stadium acts to indie singer-songwriters, musicians have pioneered ways of sparking passion, building awareness, and catalyzing engagement. Now imagine if social movements—from the fight to protect the planet to campaigns promoting global health or LGBTQIA+ rights— had the same fervent support as your favorite artists.

Adam Met, climate advocate, educator, and member of the multiplatinum band AJR, gained firsthand experience growing an audience from the ground up as the band progressed from playing in living rooms to selling out arenas. With award-winning journalist Heather Landy, Met shows how to apply fan-building strategies to social movements in exciting, inventive ways. *Amplify* is a playbook for developing passionate supporters (i.e., fans) utilizing the art and science of engagement, collaboration, and authentic connection, with tactics that will inspire people to carry your message to the world and spur others to act.

Amplify's innovative tool kit will help you find your voice and maximize your impact in the world of social progress to create the change you want to see.

Amplify

Amplify

How to Use the Power of Connection to Engage,
Take Action, and Build a Better World

Adam Met, PhD
WITH HEATHER LANDY

HARMONY

New York

Harmony Books
An imprint of Random House
A division of Penguin Random House LLC
1745 Broadway, New York, NY 10019
HarmonyBooks.com | RandomHouseBooks.com
penguinrandomhouse.com

Library of Congress Cataloging-in-Publication Data
Names: Met, Adam, 1990- author. | Landy, Heather, other.
Title: Amplify / by Adam Met with Heather Landy.
Description: New York, NY : Harmony, [2025] | Includes bibliographical references and index.
Identifiers: LCCN 2024054279 (print) | LCCN 2024054280 (ebook) |
ISBN 9780593735909 (hardcover) | ISBN 9780593735909 (ebook)
Subjects: LCSH: Social movements. | Social change. | Musicians—Political activity.
Classification: LCC HM881 .M47 2025 (print) | LCC HM881 (ebook) |
DDC 303.48/4—dc23/eng/20250107
LC record available at https://lccn.loc.gov/2024054279
LC ebook record available at https://lccn.loc.gov/2024054280

ISBN 978-0-593-73590-9
Ebook ISBN 978-0-593-73591-6

Printed in the United States of America on acid-free paper

1st Printing

First Edition

BOOK TEAM: Production editor: Andy Lefkowitz • Managing editor: Allison Fox •
Production manager: Angela McNally • Copy editor: Lawrence Krauser •
Proofreaders: Dan Goff, Karina Jha, Taylor McGowan, and Robin Slutzky

Book design by Debbie Glasserman

The authorized representative in the EU for product safety and compliance is
Penguin Random House Ireland, Morrison Chambers, 32 Nassau Street,
Dublin D02 YH68, Ireland. https://eu-contact.penguin.ie

Foreword

MAXWELL FROST

The week before I turned sixteen, I traveled to Washington, D.C., and spent a morning on a small parade float connected to a Ford F-150, standing behind a set of Tito Puente Matador Timbales. As a kid from Florida, I'm sure I didn't love the 40-degree January weather, but I don't remember the cold. What I remember is my heart pounding with excitement. It was 2013, Barack Obama was about to start his second White House term, and I was with my best friends from school, thrilled to be playing in the first salsa band ever to perform in a presidential inaugural parade.

From a young age, music was my passion. My dad is a working musician, heavily trained in both classical and contemporary music, as well as studio engineering. There was a music studio in the middle of the house where I grew up. Some of my most vivid memories are of accompanying my dad to his gigs, sometimes even performing with him. I'd watch with admiration as he'd walk up to his steel pans and transform an audience. My dad is a powerhouse, able to turn a group of people sitting around, barely paying attention, into a joyful, dancing crowd. I always loved watching how his music brought people together and made them feel something.

I attended the Osceola County School for the Arts for middle and high school, where my life revolved around playing the drums and putting together shows—passions that soon became intertwined with a budding interest in social advocacy.

The 2012 mass shooting in Connecticut at Sandy Hook Elementary School changed me. In Washington, I attended a vigil and memorial for the twenty children and six staff who lost their lives, and spent time with the families who had just lost their loved ones. We met with legislators, volunteered at local schools, and strategized on how to win common-sense gun laws. That experience instantly turned me into a passionate advocate for ending gun violence. But I wasn't very practiced at organizing—not yet.

In 2014, Bruno Mars performed in the NFL Super Bowl halftime show. Wow, that show changed my life. I watched it about a hundred times in a matter of weeks. Then I decided to re-create the show at my high school during lunchtime. I put together a band, dancers, and a team to hand out flyers to invite students to the performance. We picked high-traffic areas around the school to excite everyone about the show and used social media to ensure the details were shared in specific group chats. I didn't understand this then, but looking back, it's very clear: We were organizing.

I loved every aspect of it, from setting up the stage to figuring out the lighting and brainstorming with my friends on how to make it feel like a truly special event. For me, it wasn't just about the music; it was about creating an experience and a sense of community. That's how I learned the power of building a base. A base of supporters isn't just a collection of people who like your music or your cause; it's a network of people who share a vision and a deep commitment to something bigger than themselves.

Soon I was organizing events for even bigger communities. In 2015 my friends and I started MadSoul Music & Arts Festival, an annual Central Florida event that blends music with social advocacy. People come to hear their favorite bands, but they also get to learn about important local causes and hear from inspiring leaders. In 2024, more than 3,500 people attended MadSoul. Many of them had never been to a political event before but left inspired to act. It always felt magical to me to see people come together around a shared passion for music and a commitment, however new, to making a difference.

As I got older, I started noticing more commonalities between music and social advocacy. For example, both are rooted in storytelling and rely on the power of a well-crafted narrative. It's a way of connecting with people on a personal level to ultimately build a culture—and out of that culture based on the power of stories comes a movement. This movement might be referred to in different ways, depending on the context. You might call it a following, a support base, or a fandom.

For generations, music has been a powerful tool of resistance and change. From the anthems of the Civil Rights movement to the massive Live Aid concert that mobilized the world to address a famine in Ethiopia, music has been more than a soundtrack to change. It has brought people together to join voices, raise money, advocate for causes, and inspire action. Artists themselves have played key roles in many social movements. They played a major part in spreading awareness and galvanizing global support to fight apartheid in South Africa; they helped erase stigma during the AIDS epidemic, educating the public about the disease while raising funds for research and treatment.

While I could clearly see the commonalities and intersections between music and movements, politics still struck me as a completely separate matter, a different game with different rules. After I became the organizing director of March for Our Lives, I quickly began to see how these things were much more similar than I had ever thought. Suddenly I understood how I could use the skills I had developed as a musician growing a fan base, and as an Organizer building a movement, to make a real difference in the political arena.

At the age of twenty-four, I ran for Congress. The field of ten candidates included several veteran politicians. I knew I'd have to be creative and build not just a political campaign, but a movement. And lucky for me, I'd spent years practicing how to do just that.

As a musician, I had learned how to build fan bases, organize events, perfect my craft, and tell stories through art. As an Organizer, I had learned how to build a volunteer base, raise resources for our work, and use my story to inspire others to get involved in the fight. I applied everything I had learned in both arenas to start a political movement in Orlando, Florida, and bring people together around a shared vision. Through stories and art, we created a culture; through that culture, we created a community.

A few months into the campaign, we turned the flatbed of a trailer into a mobile stage for the Orlando Pride parade. I asked a few performer friends to join me, and we put on a mobile concert that introduced me to a large slice of the local LGBTQIA+ community. As unusually young as I was for a Congressional candidate, I wanted to show the district that supporting me was worthwhile not because my campaign was so different, but because we made things feel so familiar. As our truck went by each section of the crowd, everyone watching was briefly part of our movement. And the excitement we generated drove many to support me in the race. I won the election and became the first Gen-Z member of Congress.

Who knows what else we can achieve when arts and advocacy intertwine in new ways to create community? That's why I believe it's important that artists, fans, supporters, producers, and organizers understand the less obvious but extremely important connections between the arts and social change. Books like *Amplify* can help with this.

I've known Adam Met since I worked with March for Our Lives; he's always been a staunch supporter of that movement. When I met him, he had a very full plate, balancing a successful band, a PhD in international human rights law and sustainable development, and a nonprofit organization for climate research and advocacy. I very much admired and understood his journey. When I heard from Adam that he was working on a book to share his experiences in how he combined his passions, I knew instantly it would be an important read for artists, fans, and Organizers alike.

Amplify uncovers, explains, and celebrates the connections between music and social movements. It reminds us that we can and should use the skills and passion we learn from working in the arts to help make a positive difference in our communities. Not only is it a practical guide to getting engaged and bringing others along for the ride, it challenges us to build movements for transformational change. And it reminds us that these two worlds of music and movements, although not identical, are truly indivisible in the fight for justice and social progress.

Contents

Introduction

When my brothers and I started our band, AJR, we didn't know the "right" way to do anything. We had no industry connections. We barely had money for instruments, let alone expensive studio time. Every song on our first album was written, produced, and mixed in our parents' living room. There was no label, no team, no publicist, no agent. We learned how to do every job since there was no one else to do it, which helped us understand exactly what we needed when we were finally ready to hire people to join our scrappy team. At the time, the do-it-yourself approach was unusual in the music industry. Streaming hadn't completely upended the economics of the record business, and music production software for the masses wasn't yet as massive as it soon would become. We were a bit of an anomaly, which meant that while we were able to borrow some of the industry's tried-and-true methods for catching on with a fan base, we often had no choice but to invent our own strategies.

A good number of our ideas worked out, and a good number

didn't. We were making everything up as we went along. But it was always with the constant forethought to invest in ourselves and the mission, and never with the sense that there was just one set of rules to follow if we wanted to succeed.

We discovered early on that when you're organizing concert tours or album releases, you need tools for reaching people, tactics for mobilizing them, and ways to measure your success. We found, or built, all of these things, and it created one of the strongest, most identifiable fan bases in alt-pop, which in turn allowed us to play our music to sold-out crowds at shows around the world.

As AJR found its footing, I spent more time on pursuits outside of music. Growing up in New York City, where activism has been part of the local fabric for centuries, I was constantly aware of the many worthy yet struggling social causes that needed more people, more money, and more action. I found my home in climate work. I started a nonprofit for climate research and advocacy, earned my PhD in human rights law and sustainability, and entered the wild world of federal energy policy, all with an eye toward contributing in whatever way I could to our shift away from fossil fuels and a carbon-based economy.

As I drew closer to the world of movements for social change, I often wondered: What if important causes—like climate action or gun control or gender equality—could attract support with the breadth and intensity of a fan base? What if social change movements could rely not only on donors and occasional demonstrators but on the unique powers of a fandom?

There are lots of ways that fan bases come together, and we'll explore several of those methods in this book. The main reason these strategies work is that ultimately, we all want to be part of something larger than ourselves. In music, that larger thing is typically a collective appreciation for a particular genre or artist. But the same dynamic can be found in collective action taken up in support of a good cause.

At nearly every speech, concert, or rally I go to, fans ask me for help to find their place in the fight for social change. They want to build a better, more just world, but they don't know where to start or how they can best contribute. The first two chapters of this book are designed to help with that. After that, we get tactical about building the fan base. Growth of a movement is usually the responsibility of movement leaders, but if they borrow the lessons of the music industry, they'll see how much of this work can be carried out by the fan base itself.

WHAT EVERY CAMPAIGN NEEDS

There's a typical path for developing social movements that deliver concrete change, and it can be applied at every level, whether you're thinking about a movement on the whole (i.e., a broad effort with an overarching mission, like the climate movement); a campaign (a targeted action with concrete objectives, such as closing down a coal plant); or specific actions that make up a campaign (organizing a community protest opposing the coal plant). This path is based on decades of social-science research and practical application, and usually it looks something like this:

1. Define the change you want to see
2. Decide how you'll measure success
3. Identify the levers you'll need to pull to get there
4. Understand the audiences that can help you reach those levers
5. Develop ways to engage those audiences

6. Take action to move the levers
7. Evaluate each action's effectiveness
8. Determine how to do better next time or what to do next

There's no shortage of dreamers spinning up visions of a better world (step one), and no shortage of data to help us with steps two through four. But too many movements get hung up at step five, failing to find audiences that are big enough, or involved deeply enough, to deliver change at the required speed and scale. Climate change, human rights, gender equality, gun control, immigration reform, healthcare access, school improvements—we are moving too slowly on all of it, without the full engagement of the critical mass we need.

The music business, meanwhile, excels at reaching, developing, and engaging audiences. It starts with the songs, of course. But the industry also employs an impressive range of promotion tools and campaign tactics to get songs in front of listeners, turn listeners into fans, and turn groups of fans into thriving communities with popular and diverse participation.

The central argument of this book is that the proven tactics musicians use to grow their fan bases can be put to work building stronger support for social change. It's a multidisciplinary approach, which is how I was trained in graduate school to study problems, and how I find inspiration when it comes time to solve them. Borrowing ideas from one realm and applying them to another always involves a bit of calculated risk-taking. The math should be simple in this case, considering what's at stake. That's not meant to sound alarmist; if alarmism were a sufficient strategy, surely we would be much further ahead than we currently are on addressing climate change or protecting abortion access or closing educational gaps, or any number of other important issues. What I mean to say is that our efforts to date, while not for naught, have not been enough to forge all of the concrete changes we need. So let's try something different.

WAY UP WE GO

In 2017, AJR wrote a song called "Burn the House Down." It wasn't a political song, and it wasn't written as an anthem for any particular cause. It was simply a reflection on the incredible power and potential of millennials and Gen Z to organize and press for change.

> *Should I hang my head low?*
> *Should I bite my tongue?*
> *Or should I march with every stranger from Twitter to get shit done?*
> *Used to hang my head low*
> *Now I hear it loud*
> *Every stranger from Twitter is gonna burn this down*

The song was released in March 2018, just one month after a nineteen-year-old gunman murdered seventeen students and staff at Marjory Stoneman Douglas High School in Parkland, Florida. In the wake of the shooting, student survivors David and Lauren Hogg, X González, Cameron Kasky, Jaclyn Corin, Alex Wind, and others formed a new protest and advocacy group calling for gun control. They could have joined up with one of several established organizations working to reduce gun violence. But if school shootings were going to continue to be an epidemic, maybe it was time for students to get a voice in the movement. When the organizers of March for Our Lives asked us to perform at a rally in New York City, we jumped at the chance, eager to offer whatever we could to support their mission. We ended our set with "Burn the House Down," which by then had become a soundtrack for the group's demonstrations and public service announcements. They even played it, loudly, in the halls of Congress as they descended on Capitol Hill to meet with legislators and demand change. At the end of their New York rally, we invited the students to come up onstage and sing with us. The emotional moment gave me a new perspective on what music can do to galvanize a movement. Here were kids, literal kids, who had been through an unimaginable terror, and who were now singing and dancing in solidarity with one another and their supporters while fighting for the future they knew they deserved. For the first time, I understood what the idea of music as protest really meant.

Still, I always felt there was more I should do, and could do, for the intelligent, passionate young organizers I met that day, and for their peers pushing us toward progress on so many other worthy causes. The strategies I offer in this book are for them—and for any young person just starting out as an agent of social change. But even old hands at this type of work will find fresh ideas here for building connections, telling powerful stories, engaging trusted messengers, maximizing different platforms, finding new audiences, activating communities, and setting long-term goals.

I'm aware that even with my academic credentials and sleeves-rolled-up policy work, plenty of people see me as just another musician with another hollow agenda. My friends remind me of it, too. "Every musician has a cause," they say. "They want to make it look as if they're doing something good for the world." There may be some truth to that. But if I can't convince you that I understand the finer points of permitting-rules for energy plants on federally leased land, or of stakeholder rights for indigenous communities, I at least should be able to show you footage of fans singing or cheering or crying at our concerts—or coming up to us in airports or at meet-and-greets and sharing extraordinary stories about how our music helped them in some way—and convince you that I know something about moving people. And that's ultimately what this book is about: how to move people.

Incidentally, we're going to need a lot more people to be moved to fight for social progress on any number of fronts. We can already see that climate change is not being adequately addressed anywhere on the planet, and that the consequences of this are becoming more dire. We are also watching as America's first real momentum in decades on racial justice is getting undermined by political attacks on diversity, equity, and inclusion efforts. We are witnessing assaults on women's rights, even in places that used to protect them. We know that politicians at every level of government feel more emboldened now to exert frightening tendencies toward totalitarianism. We sense that social media platforms, which once served as exciting new organizing tools for movements like the Arab Spring and Black Lives Matter, are aging poorly and need to be revamped, reformed, or replaced.

The strategies examined in this book won't fix all of that. But they should provide a new type of blueprint for inspiring and mobilizing people who can help solve these problems. And by "people," I mean *you*, along with everyone you can then inspire and mobilize to join the causes you care about. I'm not here to tell you which causes those should be (although in Chapter One you'll find some helpful ways of thinking through the options). What I'm here to tell you, as someone lucky enough to have a night job playing music for some pretty incredible crowds, is that there is nothing like the energy of a great fan base. Every good cause should have one at its side. Building a great fan base takes time, effort, and a mix of tactics that will engage people in meaningful ways. This book distills everything I've learned over the better part of two decades about bringing people into the fold, making them feel something, and moving them to action.

Now let's dive in.

Amplify

THAT THING YOU DO

WHAT WILL YOU CHOOSE TO TAKE ACTION ON?

We have to imagine this world we need to be rushing towards.
We're not going to get there as urgently as we need to unless we
    actually want to.
And of course we need to want to, because it's going to be a much
    healthier world.
We're going to have a lovely greening of cities.
We're going to have these new jobs that are going to be so much better.
We're going to hear the birds singing.
We're going to have a more equal world.
We can't get there fast enough.

—MARY ROBINSON, FORMER PRESIDENT OF IRELAND AND FORMER
UN HIGH COMMISSIONER FOR HUMAN RIGHTS[1]

I was never meant to be a musician. Yes, I'm the bassist in a reasonably successful band. Our music has been streamed billions of times, we've played sold-out shows at Madison Square Garden, and our songs have gone platinum and double-platinum and triple-platinum. It's not what I ever thought I would be doing with my life, though. Don't get me wrong. I am thrilled, and so thankful, that this is what I do. But I wasn't meant to be a musician. I'm not even particularly good at the bass. I am not good at songwriting. I am not good at producing. I am definitely not a lead singer. For these reasons and more, it took some time for me to figure out my place in

AJR, the band my brothers and I started as teenagers. And it took me even longer to find my place in the broader music industry.

I may have complicated the process by embarking on a PhD in human rights law and sustainability, and starting a climate nonprofit, just as the band was really getting off the ground. At times, these things took up focus I otherwise might have devoted to, say, becoming a better bass player. But it was because of these other pursuits that I finally understood why my music career really mattered.

The first speech I was ever invited to give about climate action was at a rally in Omaha in 2018. I was really excited for the opportunity. I talked about regenerative agriculture (a key issue in Nebraska) and the power that individuals have to make systemic change. After the speech, I got lots of requests to take photos, but no questions or compliments about anything I had said. Feeling a bit deflated, I went back to the nearby concert venue where we were playing that night for a few thousand people and got ready for the show.

The next morning I was sitting in the Omaha airport when I was approached by a mother and daughter holding hands. The girl couldn't have been more than ten and was eagerly bouncing on her heels. "Thank you so much for yesterday," the mother said. I smiled and thanked them back and inquired about their favorite part of the show. Confused looks crossed both of their faces. "What show?" they asked. Apparently I was the confused one. They went on to tell me how inspired they were by my speech about taking action. They weren't aware of the band and didn't know we had played a concert the night before. After the rally, they said, they went home to research new ways of farming and how Nebraska could be a leader in fighting climate change.

This was the first time that being a musician felt right to me. Music was what had brought me to this place, a long way from my home in New York City. I like music; it fills me with passion and excitement. But it is only one part of the equation. I told you I was never meant to be a musician. More accurately, I was never meant to be *just* a musician. I love being onstage, guiding people toward an understanding of something, helping them feel things that compel them to cheer or cry or laugh or widen their eyes in surprise. I love participating in the act of moving people. But I couldn't be effective at that, whether as a musician or as a climate advocate, until I found my own place, a place that actually felt right.

Some days it's still a struggle. In the years since that speech in Omaha, I finished my PhD, became a development advocate for the United Nations, formulated new approaches to energy policy that got Republicans and Democrats in Congress to shake hands, taught climate advocacy at Columbia University. And still, when I want to talk to people about urban farming practices or energy plant permits, they want to hear about what it was like performing at Red Rocks Amphitheatre.

I understand why people have a hard time seeing me the way I want to be seen. I've spent more than eighteen years now working to set up the tours, the stories, the games, the community, and the emotional connections that created a fan base for the music. I haven't yet spent the same amount of time or energy making people care about the environment, or the specific things I've had to say about it. Also, I haven't really applied the same fan-building tactics to move people to action on climate or other important issues.

But what if we could?

WHAT'S YOUR THING?

On a wet April morning, a few hours before a big show in Charlotte, North Carolina, I made my way to nearby Davidson College. I'd agreed to give a talk there about climate policy because I'm deeply worried about the future of our planet, and because I was curious what the atmosphere was like on a college campus in a swing state in 2024, and because the student group that invited me figured people would show up to meet the "A" in AJR. So that was how I introduced myself: I gave the students all the reasons why I was there. After highlighting several big climate policy wins under the Biden administration, I asked who in the room was majoring in something connected to climate. Hardly anyone said yes. So I started cold-calling on students to ask them what they were studying. Engineering, education, marketing, visual arts, international relations, political science—they didn't see how any of it related directly to climate. One student told me he was taking architecture classes. I asked if he could imagine working with sustainable materials, or designing buildings to withstand increasingly severe weather events. I inquired whether the pre-med students had learned about the mosquito-borne illnesses that will spread with the Earth's temperature rise. I challenged the business majors to think about ways for industries to adapt to a warming planet, as nearly every sector will eventually have to do.

Maybe you saw these connections coming. Maybe you've already made connections like this for yourself and have joined the movement, or at least can see a pathway for doing so. Or maybe climate change isn't the issue that speaks loudest to you. In fact, the world is full of pressing problems in need of broad-based solutions. We could apply this same exercise to any of them. We also could look at other ways, aside from schooling or professional expertise, to contribute to social change, whether through your money, your time, your vote, your affiliation with an organization that's already doing great work, or your idea for starting a new campaign. But first, you need to know which issue you're focusing on. So what will it be? How do you find *your* thing?

While I could easily argue that climate change touches just about everything (from the energy we create, to the way we travel, to the things we make, eat, wear, and throw away), I promise I won't be too disappointed if your cause of choice isn't climate. Throughout this book, you'll hear from leaders of movements for gun regulation, global health, racial equality, immigrant justice, LGBTQIA+ rights, and more. They're all doing important, inspiring work and asking crucial questions about how to get more support for the changes they want to see in the world. In later chapters, we'll explore specific tactics for building fan bases for causes. But first we need to make sure everyone can envision a path to participating in social change, which starts with understanding how a path might materialize in the first place. My own path, the one that led me to climate advocacy, was shaped by a well-timed field trip, a picky PhD adviser, and a purple Nintendo Game Boy Color I got when I was in fourth grade. So let's start there.

HERE'S TO YOU, MRS. ROBINSON

In my senior year of high school, I went on a class trip to see a presentation by Mary Robinson, the former president of Ireland and a past UN high commissioner for human rights. I was excited to go, because I liked field trips. I came home with a newfound appreciation for the relationship between human dignity and the environment, and with a mini-crush on the person who'd imparted this knowledge with warmth and certainty and a charming Irish lilt. I went on to learn everything I could about her work, including the fact that she saw herself as a latecomer to the climate movement, and that she regretted not realizing earlier the impact of climate on basic human rights like access to food, water, and sanitation. I found it fascinating that a person could help usher in as much social change as she had—it was during her presidency that Ireland decriminalized homosexuality, legalized contraception and divorce, established the right to legal aid in civil cases, and started including women on juries—and all the while she was still seeking the right place for herself in the fight for progress. As Mary would tell me years later, when I interviewed her on a podcast:

> You know, I spent my five years as UN high commissioner for human rights and I knew there was another part of the UN dealing with climate, the climate convention, and I didn't make the connection to human rights. It was afterwards, working in African countries on economic and social rights, that literally my eyes were opened in a very humiliating way, in a humbling way. I had missed it. And so I'm a latecomer, in that sense, to the connection. But once I got it, I really got it.[2]

And luckily, she got it in time for me to first hear about it when I was an impressionable seventeen-year-old. Prior to hearing Mary speak, news reports about a famine in one country or a flood in another felt unreal to me, or at least very distant from life at home in America. But now, using the Universal Declaration of Human Rights as a framework for thinking about the protection and sanctity of all individuals, I could break down the boundaries between the society I was living in and the places taking the brunt of our escalating climate crisis. And of course it wouldn't be long before America, too, was noticeably suffering the effects of the Earth's temperature rise.

EVOLUTION, EFFECTIVENESS, AND RENEWABLE ENERGY

The same year I took that field trip, I also visited Valley Windworks. That was the name of the giant wind-power plant taken over by Team Galactic in Pokémon Diamond. I'd been playing Pokémon in varying iterations since I was nine years old, first on my purple Game Boy Color, then on a Nintendo DS, and then on a Nintendo Switch. Even now I play it from time to time out of nostalgia, and also because it still feels like an escape. As a kid, as my little life got more complicated with new offshoot paths to consider and decisions to make, I appreciated the game's linearity. I never had to wonder what to do or how to do it, because it was all laid out for me. I just had to complete the task at hand and move on to the next one. As an adult, I appreciate this feeling all the more.

Energy was always part of the storyline in Pokémon, whether in fueling the characters for their battles or in the development of the different towns and continents featured in the game. A magnetic train appeared in Pokémon early on. Valley Windworks showed up in generation four of the series; other generations brought us the Kalos solar energy plant and a geothermal plant on Blush Mountain. I can't say I knew much about renewable energy prior to any of that. I just knew it was an important consideration for the survival of a world I was building and wouldn't have minded living in from time to time.

BACK ON THE CLIMATE BUS

After I finished high school in 2008, with my Nintendo close at hand and memories of Mary's talk still fresh in my mind, it took a decade for climate issues to figure prominently again on my radar screen. In the interim, I studied business and philosophy as an undergraduate and took courses in sustainable development; after that, I got a master's in constitutional religious law and was accepted into a PhD program. My PhD adviser was decidedly *not* into my idea of exploring the implications for human rights in space (yes, that really was my initial proposal), so I started researching the intersection of human rights and commercial development back here on Earth. Meanwhile, on the AJR side of things, my brothers and I had signed with a manager, released two full-length albums (*Living Room* and *The Click*), and started touring as much as we could. And that's how I ended up on a tour bus in San Francisco in 2018, with a bunch of tired musicians and an apocalyptic vision of our climate future.

We were heading up to the Bay Area after a show in Los Angeles. It was the middle of the night, and we were all asleep when the air conditioner suddenly turned off. With twelve people on board and hardly any space in our narrow, stuffy sleeping compartments, it got hot very quickly. We all woke up sweaty and went to the front of the bus, where our tour manager, Keith, told us that because of forest fires, thick smoke had settled into the Bay Area. It would be too unhealthy to pull air from outside into the AC system.

An hour later, we pulled up to the Masonic, an auditorium in San Francisco's Nob Hill neighborhood. Like the rest of the city, it was shrouded in smoke. Keith made us put on firefighter-style gas masks for the short walk to the building entrance. We loaded into the venue quickly and were alarmed to hear there were already fans lined up outside for that evening's show. We opened the doors many hours early, allowing everyone to escape the choking air and wait inside as we finished setting up. This was the first time I ever felt directly affected by climate change. I wondered if it was the beginning of a new era for how we thought about touring and the fan experience.

It turns out 2018 was a historically destructive year for California wildfires. But it wasn't a fluke. Even more acreage burned in

2020, and again in 2021.[3] And California would be far from the only place to keep breaking records for extreme events tied to climate change.

CAUSE FATIGUE

Caring about climate change, or any intractable problem, can easily get exhausting. The fatigue might set in after years of fighting, but it also can arrive early on. After my eye-opening experience talking with students at Davidson College about what they were studying, I visited several more campuses during AJR's 2024 concert tour. At Grand Valley State University near Grand Rapids, Michigan, one of the students in the room told me he'd been heavily involved in climate action during high school but was disillusioned by Big Oil's emphasis on carbon capture. The technology, which is still years if not decades away from being economically viable to use at scale, collects and stores the carbon dioxide released by burning fossil fuels. Necessary as it may be to a holistic response to the climate crisis, investing in carbon capture allows the oil and gas industry to claim it's helping to solve climate change even as it conveniently continues extracting fossil fuels from the Earth.

When any of us, but young people especially, start focusing on solutions that are that complex, that controversial, and that far in the future, the problem quickly gets overwhelming. Hearing this student talk about how depressed and burned out he was, I tried to bring the discussion back to a place where he could see the impact he could have. I pointed out that there are many solutions already available to us: renewable energy; regenerative agriculture; mitigation projects, like the Billion Oyster Project in New York City to restore protective reefs in New York Harbor, or the city of Grand Rapids's own curb-cut rain gardens to capture and treat stormwater that might otherwise pollute local creeks.[4] I don't know if I convinced him to give the movement another shot. I hope he at least understands he's not alone in his feelings of discouragement.

I give myself similar reminders from time to time, because I'm as prone to paralysis as anyone else. In 2017, Donald Trump revoked the country's support for the historic Paris Agreement on climate change soon after he was sworn into the White House. Over the next four years, he proceeded to roll back more than a hundred environmental rules that had been put in place to protect our air and water, preserve land and wildlife, and decrease the greenhouse gas emissions causing global warming.[5] I was just beginning to get more involved in the climate movement during this time. Many times I wondered if I should even bother, given that literally every other week, on average, the Trump administration was doing something to undermine measures that were already in place to protect the planet. In late 2024, I had to wonder again, as Trump was reelected.

It's painful to think about how much potential for social change has been lost to the very real effects of outrage fatigue and general disillusionment. Efrén Olivares, whose work you'll learn more about in Chapter Five, arrived in the United States from Mexico at age thirteen already knowing he wanted to be a lawyer. His college courses in political science and philosophy had him questioning the ways in which societies get organized, and his career aspirations coalesced around social justice. While in law school, he took a summer internship as a civil rights observer in Chiapas, in southern Mexico, where a new hydroelectric plant was being planned. He watched as indigenous men were falsely accused of crimes so that they would be pressured to agree to the project, if not entirely dispossessed of their homes and property to make way for it. I'll let Efrén tell you the effect this had on him as a law student:

It was almost the reason I decided not to be involved in this type of work. The inequality and inequity is so structured and entrenched. There was always an economic interest, typically a transnational economic interest, at play. I wondered, is there anything I can even do to make a dent? But I ultimately decided to give it a shot.

I'd argue it was too close a call, given the important immigrant-justice advocacy work he went on to do at organizations like the Texas Civil Rights Project and the Southern Poverty Law Center.

TWO STEPS FORWARD, ONE STEP BACK

The summer that George Floyd was killed in Minneapolis, Chi Ossé was twenty-two years old and completely unsure what his future would hold. He'd been working in New York's nightlife industry until the sector evaporated in the Covid-19 pandemic. Now he was isolated at home in Crown Heights, the Brooklyn neighborhood where he had grown up, spending way too much time on his phone. One day he started seeing video footage of a Black man pinned by a white police officer, a knee to his neck. The man was murdered right there on the street. Angry in a more visceral way than he had ever been about previous police killings he had seen on the news, and in search of like-minded people to commune with, Chi ended his Covid-19 quarantine and went to a demonstration outside the Barclays Center arena in Brooklyn, where he got pepper-sprayed by police as the scene turned violent. On Instagram Live, he did his best to document what he described as "state-sanctioned violence that was being enacted upon nonviolent protesters." It was the first time he had ever taken part in a demonstration.

Chi kept turning out on the streets, and he started speaking at some of the protests. He was soaking up all the information he could about police funding—who controls it, what it costs, how to reduce it—and meeting other young demonstrators. They set up an encampment outside City Hall that summer, pressuring the city council to vote against New York's roughly $100 billion city budget and reallocate police funding to education and mental health programs. Chi said he was "enthralled" to be part of what he saw as a high point of the movement to defund the police, and he was heartbroken when the city budget was approved with none of the changes the protesters had sought. As he told me:

> I think it really changed the course in terms of how the movement progressed and ended up, but it also changed something in me. I was so annoyed at the fact that there are these individuals who represent us, who couldn't even listen to this large movement of people who were making what I perceived to be a pretty decent ask based off of the events that took place. I wanted to change something about that. I went home and I was just like, I need to run for office and be that person who's in there, who can make those decisions, because I feel like I would be more principled in my understanding of not only this moment, but of the issues that my generation—and my community, my neighbors, my family—care about.

Less than two weeks later, Chi declared his candidacy. He was running for city council. At twenty-two, he had no political experience, but he had amassed a decent-size social media following while speaking at the protests, and he understood the aesthetics of a modern campaign. He used eye-catching graphics in his posts, he got a friend who now works at *GQ* to help style him for events, and he was written up in publications like *Vogue* and *Paper*. None of this was typical for a New York City Council race. When someone in Chi's camp compared the campaign to an album rollout, he understood the analogy. His late father, Reginald Ossé, was a lawyer for Def Jam Recordings and was later known for interviewing hip-hop icons on his popular podcast *The Combat Jack Show*;[6] and Chi's maternal grandfather was a Grammy-winning music producer who worked with R&B superstar Luther Vandross.[7]

On January 1, 2022, the New York City Council inaugurated its youngest ever member and its first from Gen Z.[8] Like a handful of other progressives who won that year, Chi came into office hopeful that his election represented a tipping point, and that the next budget, with the police department allocation he campaigned against, would fail. It didn't, though.

> I ended up being one of six council members who voted against this budget, out of fifty-one members, and that was just an eye-opening experience and disappointment, because I really came in with that optimism. And while that was hurtful to see, I think it really matured me. It really helped me recalibrate what change looks like and how to create that change.

Chi didn't stop speaking out against police funding. But he quickly pivoted to issues where he suspected he could be more productive as a council member, taking up matters of housing, healthcare, and education. The path that led him into the streets and then into office would simply have to widen.

WHAT CAN I DO?

Some people look at a vexing social problem, like Chi did, and earnestly ask, "What can I *do*?" Others have almost the same exact response, but with the intonation of the shrug emoji: "Eh. What can *I* do?" My advice in both cases is the same:

- Stop thinking in terms of individual action. What most causes need instead are acts of individual leadership that inspire *collective* action. If you're worried about climate change and your plan is to personally switch from plastic straws to paper, well, that's not going to have much effect on anything besides making your iced coffee harder to sip as the top of your straw gets soggy. But if you start a campaign to eliminate all single-use plastic in your school district or community, now you've exponentially expanded your potential impact.

- Vote. I know, I know. This is an individual action—but only when you're inside the voting booth. Research the candidates and discuss the options with family, friends, and neighbors. This is especially crucial for local elections, which almost never get the attention they're due and yet can have real impact on important social issues. (Kids—you can play a valuable role here, too! Find out which candidates align with your cause, and make a presentation for your parents about it.) In our polarized society, these kinds of kitchen-table discussions remain an influential factor in elections.

- To act globally, think locally. The whole purpose of advocacy is to fight for something concrete, something specific. One of the best ways to do that is to engage people on an issue in their own community and convince them to do something about it. That's not to say you shouldn't care about people or problems in other places. But if you're not sure how to get involved in social change, or where to begin tackling a global issue like climate or poverty or gender inequality, thinking about it locally is a good start—and the solutions you find close to home might be easily replicable elsewhere. Maybe environmental justice is important to you, and so you study the topic in school and look into established organizations doing work on the issue; maybe you even travel halfway across the country to protest a pipeline or lobby a statehouse for an environmental cleanup bill. Or . . . maybe there's a problem with pollution from an industrial plant right in your community and so you start a campaign with your neighbors, drafting letters and making signs in someone's basement to urge the closing of the facility. In that case, you're probably thinking about the problem in terms of pollution, not environmental justice or the climate movement writ large. But those grassroots actions now make you one small but vital part of a global movement.

AN EXERCISE BEFORE WE MOVE ON

If you're still looking for a path into social change, try this thought experiment:

In your ideal world, what do cities look like? What do financial systems look like? What about parks? Schools? Transit systems? How do people treat one another? How do they get their food? Where do they go for medical care? Feel free to add and answer any other important questions you'd want to see addressed and resolved in your utopian society. Make sure everything is framed in positive terms, i.e., as things you want to see, not as things you don't want to see. Think about the solution instead of the problem. Instead of envisioning "no capitalism," describe the economic system that your ideal world would use.

If you could realize your vision for just one of those areas, but everything else about your world would look exactly the same as it does in our existing world, which category would you choose? And if you knew you could eventually realize *all* of your goals, which one would you want to see realized first?

Hopefully now you're zeroing in on the kind of change in the world that's important to you. But maybe you're still wondering about the role you'll play in bringing that change to life. Don't worry. We'll get to that next, in Chapter Two.

WHO ARE YOU?

FINDING YOUR ROLE IN THE FIGHT FOR SOCIAL PROGRESS

I already admitted to you at the top of Chapter One that I'm not a great bass player. Now I'd like to explain why that's the case. I chose the bass for practical reasons, not out of passion. As a kid, I was much more interested in piano, and I was actually really good at it. But my brother Ryan was even better. So when it came to deciding who would play which instruments when we started AJR, it made sense for Ryan to take the keyboard. Jack started on the drums and then picked up the guitar. That left me with the bass. I took three lessons and taught myself the rest—the rest being enough for me to competently perform AJR's songs, but not much else.

I suppose I could have spent the next few years focused on improving my bass playing, but instead I found myself gravitating toward the business side of the band. I learned the ins and outs of the radio industry, how to pick touring markets, how to price tickets using data analytics, and how to roll out an album campaign; I put my undergraduate business degree to use doing marketing, brand strategy, and development. In fact, we all ended up occupying distinct roles beyond the instruments we played, with Jack out front as lead vocalist, Ryan producing the records and collaborating with Jack on songwriting, and me overseeing our tours and business interests. Each set of responsibilities was indispensable in its own way to the growth of our fan base.

Movements, too, depend on a mix of distinct but equally vital roles. The trick for each of us, and for the causes we're aligned with, is figuring out the job in which we'll be most effective. Some of us have the vision to design campaigns or the charisma to lead them. Some of us can make more impact as financial contributors to movements. Some of us are eager to march in the streets, or are in a position to support movements through corporate partnerships or political lobbying. Or maybe we have skills in accounting, IT, graphic design, social media strategy, fundraising, publicity, or human resources management, and could put those skills to work on behalf of a cause.

It's important to note that while you might come up against certain experience-level requirements if you were to apply for certain jobs in the social impact space, your age has nothing to do with your overall efficacy as a contributor to social change. If you think you're too young to accomplish much, look at the history of the March for Our Lives campaign, whose organizers were just teenagers when they mobilized in the aftermath of an incredible trauma, and inspired thousands of local actions that were also student led. Or maybe you think you're too old to contribute to social change. In that case, have a look at Third Act, a group started by veteran climate activist Bill McKibben to engage people over the age of sixty in climate activism. Regardless of your age or experience level, there is no shortage of social change organizations that could use your time and support.

Still, the question remains: What's the right role, for you specifically, in the fight for social change? Understanding the different options is key. But first it's useful to discover some important things about yourself.

"WHO AM I TO TELL ME WHO I AM?"

I was thrilled to find out recently that popular psychology author Adam Grant is a huge fan of the AJR song "Netflix Trip," because I'm a huge fan of Adam Grant. His book *Originals* influenced how I go about building support for my own crazy ideas, while *Think Again* made me understand why it's important to reevaluate and sometimes replace my most comfortable ways of thinking, even on topics about which I presume to know a fair amount.

As an organizational psychologist, Adam thinks a lot about the various roles that make up a group, and the ways in which different personalities influence how each of those roles gets presented. So I couldn't wait to talk to him about the idea of slotting ourselves into the right roles to maximize our impact. The conversation taught me something interesting about how humans behave—and how organizations within movements can correct for it.

It turns out, most of us are shockingly bad at gauging our own strengths and weaknesses, even when we think we have it all figured out.

"Most people have some blind spots, and we normally think about that as being unaware of your weaknesses," Adam noted. But there are other, more surprising ways in which we might misgauge ourselves or our fit for a particular role. For instance, he told me, research suggests we tend to *overestimate* our abilities in areas in which our skills are poor. And when we do possess special traits or talents, we're likely to lose sight of their value precisely because they come easily to us. If you have a photographic memory, for instance, you might not consider how rare that is, because it's effortless for you. That oversight might then keep you from gravitating toward roles that capitalize on that particular skill or trait, which is a loss both for you and for a good organization that could have benefited from your unusual talent.

Those are just a couple of examples of how we commonly misjudge ourselves or our optimal roles in society. It's staggering to think about the amount of potential impact that gets lost to these kinds of mismeasurements.

"I think if you put all that together, I would be surprised if people were accurate about even fifty percent of their Achilles' heels and greatest strengths," Adam told me. "There's a lot of role mismatching that comes from that. And then there's the role mismatch problem that comes from people just gravitating toward things based on interest and enjoyment as opposed to skill. We'd like to think those things go together, but they don't always."

In other words, there are many pitfalls on the journey to finding the right roles for ourselves. Just look at Andrew Yang, who nearly skipped out on being the front person for his own presidential campaign.

UBI FOR PRESIDENT?

When Andrew, an entrepreneur turned nonprofit leader turned political candidate, launched his first (and so far only) U.S. presidential bid, he wanted to call the campaign UBI 2020, as a way of putting his universal basic income policy front and center. His pitch: Replace the usual patchwork of government welfare programs with a payment of $1,000 a month to every American, which at the time would have put nearly the entire country above the federal poverty line, while also stimulating the economy and providing a safety net for people whose jobs are lost to automation or other technology.

While the idea was drawing attention thanks to his campaign, nobody in Andrew's camp, or outside of it, cared much for his proposed UBI 2020 slogan. Here's how Andrew recalled the situation four years later, as he reflected on his experience as a political candidate:

> They thought it was a urinary tract infection or some kind of medical condition, and they didn't understand it as a presidential campaign. They said, "Look, this needs to be around a person, so we should call it Yang 2020." And the first time I heard that, I winced, because the prospect of imagining your name as the logo or brand of a campaign felt very self-promotional.

If universal basic income were a band, Andrew reluctantly became its lead singer. Like Mick Jagger with the Rolling Stones or Bono with U2, he intertwined his own identity with something even bigger than himself. All across Iowa that winter, as the primaries neared, Andrew talked about universal basic income (or "the freedom dividend," as he dubbed it) everywhere he went, and hardly anyone talked about universal basic income without also talking about Andrew.

The Yang 2020 slogan, while clearly an improvement over UBI 2020, didn't exactly deliver political victory. After getting just one percent of the vote in Iowa, Yang ended his run in New Hampshire the following week and endorsed Joe Biden,[1] who of course went on to win the Democratic nomination and the 2020 general election. But in putting his personal story front and center and allowing voters to get to know a lot more about him and his family, and then turning that connection with people into a platform for his idea, Andrew introduced millions of Americans to the concept of universal basic income; by that measure, the campaign was a big success.

DOES EVERY MOVEMENT NEED A LEADER?

Being the person out front is a heavy responsibility. You're making yourself synonymous with the idea you represent, and opening yourself to all kinds of attention. The criticism—especially online, where it can be especially hateful and frustratingly anonymous— requires an exceptionally thick skin. Even the accolades can be difficult for mere mortals to handle when they come from an army of seemingly anonymous usernames; plenty of famous people will tell you that they question the reality of positive comments when the negatives are so much more plentiful. Though we may feel little sympathy for these people, it doesn't change the fact that getting rock star treatment is not a normal way to go through life, which inevitably causes complications. This seems to be the case for both figurative and literal rock stars.

My brother Jack was the obvious person to front AJR, with his considerable vocal talent and his fearlessness onstage. As natural a fit as he is for the front role, I know it's a lot for him to shoulder. One way he copes is by wearing a trapper hat when he performs, no matter how hot the weather. The hat has become iconic to our fans. A lot of kids, and sometimes even older fans, wear the same type of hat when they come see us play. But the hat thing is really just a way for Jack to step into character as our front person. He wears it onstage and during interviews, and most fans probably wouldn't recognize him without it. (At a festival once, a young woman who spotted Ryan in the audience after our set asked for a photo and got extremely annoyed with the sweaty-haired guy next to him who kept trying to get into the frame—only it wasn't a random photo-bomber; it was Jack, hatless and apparently oblivious to his incon-spicuousness, making the not-unreasonable assumption that she wanted him in the photo as well.)

In groups like the Beatles, the Eagles, Fleetwood Mac, and Crosby, Stills, Nash & Young, the lead vocals role was shared by multiple band members. It's rarer now to find a band without a des-ignated front person, which makes sense given how important social media has become to the music industry. Fandoms are driven in large part by the connection people feel to a performer, and convey-ing a personality is far easier for an individual than a group. Bands without a recognizable leader can be a tough sell in that sense.

It's not much different for movements, which need leaders not only to devise and manage the campaigns but to serve as the face of the cause and create a critical conduit for others to learn about and connect with the issue (see: Susan B. Anthony, Martin Luther King, Jr., Nelson Mandela, and Greta Thunberg). People draw inspiration from ideas. But they *connect* to other people.

So let's get back to Andrew. As uncomfortable as he initially was with making himself the personal conduit for his ideas in his presi-dential campaign, it actually wasn't the first time he had done some-thing like this. I'll let Andrew tell you what went through his mind on the day when his advisers had to practically beg him to become the front person for his own campaign:

> It reminded me of something that a colleague of mine shared when I was running a nonprofit that I started, called Venture for America, which was founded in 2011.

We had this conversation in 2013 or so where he said,
"Anything you do for Andrew Yang elevates Venture for
America, and you should not be afraid to seek out things
that burnish your own profile, even though you might
feel self-conscious. It's not about you, it's about the mission; but you and the mission of the organization are one
and the same, and indeed, the organization cannot succeed if you don't have a certain level of exposure and no-
toriety."

So the fact that the folks who worked for me were essentially pushing me to seek out speaking opportunities
or what have you made me feel much more at ease, because I wouldn't want the people I worked with to think I
was somehow seeking the spotlight for its own sake, or
for my sake. It was for the organization's sake.

I have felt similarly sheepish about making myself the center of attention, especially in the context of advocacy or policy work. But
I'm aware my public profile as a musician draws attention to causes
that are important to me. If members of Congress can't quite separate me, or photos they've taken with me to show their kids, from
the climate advocacy work we do at Planet Reimagined, or from my
idea of co-locating renewable energy projects on federal land leased
to oil and gas companies, I'm okay with that. But getting there required some adjusting on my part, just as it did for Andrew.

Despite having seen his nonprofit benefit as he showed up on
more conference stages and started winning personal accolades for
his Venture for America work (for example, making Fast Company's 2012 list of the one hundred most creative people in business),[2]
Andrew was hesitant to front his own presidential bid, even well
after declaring his candidacy in 2018. As he told me:

For months no one knew who I was—no one cared who I was. [But] I found that the more I shared about myself, the more people began to identify with the campaign, even very, very far into the campaign. And the support for universal basic income in Iowa grew significantly, from 27 percent when we started, to 55 percent or 60 percent, and by the end of the campaign it was up to 67 percent.

The rationale [for voters] wasn't necessarily "Oh, that would really help me in my day-to-day life," or "I'd be able to pay for school supplies" or whatnot. A lot of them would say, "I heard Andrew Yang speak; I think he's onto something, and he seems to be trying to do something positive for us, so now I'm for this concept."

When I was pitching the concept, I talked in concrete terms about how it would help them. But people need a person to connect an idea to, in order to get excited about the idea. This is, by the way, not necessarily the way I want ideas to spread. I feel like an idea should just be able to stand on its own two feet, and people embrace it or don't embrace it based upon the quote-unquote merits. But that was not my experience with universal basic income.

With that connection, the public conversation around UBI didn't have to expire with Andrew's presidential bid. Had UBI 2020 been his campaign theme, that might have spelled the end for the concept as a topic of national conversation. But after he stopped being a candidate, Andrew the person was able to continue carrying the banner for the cause. He's done something similar with another plank in his 2020 campaign: ranked-choice voting, which is the other big policy issue he has been working on in recent years. In ranked-choice systems, which Andrew advocates bringing to a range of state and local elections, voters rank multiple candidates in order of preference instead of choosing just one. The system typically allows for instant run-offs between election candidates, so that if no one wins more than 50 percent of the vote, the candidate with the fewest votes gets eliminated, and whoever ranked that candidate first would then see their vote steered to their second choice. Then there's another round of counting, and the process repeats until someone can claim a majority.[3] The system neutralizes the "spoiler effect" of having similar candidates who effectively split the vote of their combined base, allowing another candidate with fewer voters to surge ahead; it's especially popular with supporters of third-party candidates, who commonly play spoiler in a system where electoral victory is based on a simple plurality.

A few years ago, Andrew was on a Zoom with fellow advocates for voter reform and came away with a sinking feeling similar to the one he'd had as a nonprofit leader, and then as a presidential candidate. "I asked them, 'Who's the most prominent political figure who has come out for ranked-choice voting?'" he recalled. "And they said, 'Probably you.'" Once again, Andrew was all but destined to become the front person for an idea he wanted to spread. "I suppose the message is that in order for universal basic income or ranked-choice voting to get to a certain place," he concluded, "you kind of need a Mr. or Mrs. Universal Basic Income or Ranked-Choice Voting."

That much is clear. But can anyone embody the role? Being a good front person requires tireless enthusiasm, natural charisma, and fearlessness in putting yourself out there to connect with people. If that's not you, don't worry. There are plenty of other roles that make crucial contributions to movements and social change. Let's take a look at a few.

TRUSTED MESSENGERS

Movements are dependent on all kinds of messengers, and not just the classic front-person type. Trusted messengers have genuine expertise in their subject area and a proven ability to inspire, educate, and communicate on behalf of a campaign or cause. They might be public educators like David Attenborough, celebrity advocates like Angelina Jolie, journalists like 1619 Project creator Nikole Hannah-Jones, or firsthand witnesses to situations that a cause or campaign is meant to address, like the students who started March for Our Lives. Whatever their connection to the message itself, they need credibility and authenticity to be trusted—and that mainly comes from the passion, rigor, and communication skills they bring to their chosen cause.

Delivering a trusted message is no easy task; often it comes down to that trite but not altogether unuseful idea of "meeting people where they are." (Personally, I prefer trying to meet people a few steps ahead of where they are, which is usually feasible so long as you make sure you're giving them the tools to get there.) Either way, you're ultimately aiming to elevate people's understanding of an issue. And sometimes that happens in unexpected ways.

In elementary school, I would always look forward to the rainy days. Instead of spending recess in the yard, we would go to the auditorium to watch videos, the most popular of which was *Bill Nye the Science Guy*. When I met Bill in person more than twenty-five years after my first exposure to his accessible, entertaining lessons in chemistry and physics, the mini-scientist in me was starstruck. Bill, who was trained as a mechanical engineer, told me that when young people come up to him and want to know how to become the next Bill Nye, he always asks: "Are you funny?" The fans never know how to respond, he said. Often, they're nerds with astrophysics de-

grees who want to become famous. This, Bill told me, is not a recipe
for success as a trusted messenger:

> As they say, when you're in love, you want to tell the
> world—and they love science. They want everybody to
> be interested in science. But a big part of the reason the
> *Science Guy* show was successful was that it was funny.
> And as I say, I have a big advantage in that I am funny-
> looking. But seriously, everybody on the crew had a ter-
> rific sense of humor, and so all those things we did were
> often, to me, very funny. I still once in a while look at an
> old segment and just crack myself up.

Sporting an oversize purple bow tie from his famously extensive
neckwear collection, Bill told me his show, which ran for six seasons
during the 1990s and won nineteen Emmy Awards, was written to
appeal to fourth graders because of "very compelling research that
fourth grade, or ten years old, was about as old as you can be to get
the lifelong passion for science." I was squarely in the target demographic for the initial run of *Science Guy* and can confirm the hold
that a wacky experiment, and silly bow tie, can have on a kid at that
age.

Bill worked at Boeing and started moonlighting as a comedian
after he won a Steve Martin look-alike contest in Seattle[4] in the late
1970s (true story, and if you look up the old photos online, you'll see
how remarkable his resemblance was back then to the famous comedy actor). Success with stand-up led to segments on local television
and then to *Bill Nye the Science Guy,* which became a staple in homes
and schools around the country because of its comedy-infused ped-
agogy. Bill knew his skills. He knew his audience. He became a
trusted messenger because of how the two came together.

Bill's fun, accessible messaging about science education turned him into a celebrity. But often this goes in reverse, and established celebrities turn into trusted messengers for a cause they've aligned themselves with. Take the example of Megan Thee Stallion. Having suffered from anxiety and depression, the popular rapper has used her platform to draw attention to mental health issues. On her website BadBitchesHaveBadDaysToo.com, she offers a sizable online directory of free mental health resources from reputable organizations, with an emphasis on programs geared toward young people, Black people, Native Americans, and the LGBTQIA+ community. She has also recorded PSAs and podcasts about mental health issues, and even raps about them in songs like 2022's "Anxiety" (which includes the line "Bad bitches have bad days too") and the 2023 track "Cobra," with its lyrics about thoughts of suicide and self-harm.

When Megan's mental health site debuted, a clinical psychologist interviewed by CNN noted the welcome contrast between the nuanced, identities-based approach it takes in offering resources, versus the less helpful "one-size-fits-all" approach commonly found on sites that aggregate mental health resources. He also praised Megan for "forcing the conversation to go mainstream."[5] Megan is a talented artist, not a trained psychologist. But it's safe to call her a trusted messenger on the issue of mental health.

UNLEASH THE RESEARCHERS

Messengers are important, but who's arming them with the accurate information and illuminating data points they'll need to persuade the masses? That would be the researchers, although the key role they play in movement-building can get a lot broader than that.

As someone who devoted several years to investigating and analyzing a topic for a PhD, I find it frustrating that so much rigorous academic work languishes on library shelves, trapped in research papers that are rarely seen or used. (Seriously, if anyone needs three hundred pages on stakeholder approaches to human rights and development in the commercial context, hit me up.) But when it's applied wisely, rigorous research can be extremely useful in the practical arts of social change. It might, for example, unlock sociological or anthropological clues that can help community organizers better understand the people they want to reach, which then allows them to craft smarter strategies. This pairing also has benefits for the researchers, who can learn a lot from organizers about why their research matters, who's affected by their findings, and how communities can alter the course of a frustrating trend line they've been on.

Good researchers wade into their subject matter with a hypothesis and allow the facts to lead them to the appropriate conclusions. That's a very different mindset from that of the organizers of campaigns or movements, who tend to have concrete goals at the outset; they want this petition signed, or that industry regulated, or those rights protected. When I started Planet Reimagined with Mila Rosenthal—a PhD in social anthropology and an adjunct professor at Columbia University, with past leadership roles at Amnesty International and the UN Development Programme—it was with an eye toward putting climate research and advocacy under one roof. But these meant different things to each of us. Mila has a long history of activism and rabble-rousing, starting when she barred the doors of Hamilton Hall at Columbia University as a student in the 1980s to protest apartheid in South Africa. This is somewhat in contrast to my own style of advocacy, which is often focused on finding the overlap between groups with seemingly disparate perspectives. This difference in approach has led to an unlikely but productive partnership between us.

Combining research with action, as we advocate for at Planet

Reimagined, is pretty unusual, especially in academia, where researchers tend to stay in their own lane. Our strategy is to bring in fellows with expertise in either research or advocacy and team them up, so that their study of problems and potential solutions in the climate space triggers ideas that can be turned into action.

ACTIVIST HISTORIANS: HOLDING US TO ACCOUNT

In the world of movements, historians might easily be lumped together with either the trusted messengers or the researchers. But there's a particular variety of historian that transcends the definition of those categories. For lack of a better term, I'll call them "activist historians." They concern themselves not only with the facts in the historical record, but with facts that might be *missing* from the historical record—and when they find them, they hold their field of study accountable for the oversight and get the record corrected. There are so many examples of society's important contributors (often women or people of color) whose work has gone undocumented or otherwise kept from view, until someone discovered the truth, or noticed a sorely missing perspective, and pointed it out to the rest of us.

At Brown University, there's a fascinating project under way to document the often overlooked contributions that women and girls have made to hip-hop since the genre's founding in the 1970s. Enongo Lumumba-Kasongo, an assistant music professor involved in the work, said the effort began after a small group of feminist hip-hop scholars encountered stark gaps in information about many of the women and girls who were involved in the genre, especially early on. In tracking down this lost history, theKEEPERS, as the project is known, is constructing both a digital archive and a commentary about gender dynamics in the music industry, and in broader society. But it starts with the piecing together of stories about individual women and girls whose contributions to hip-hop were forgotten, overlooked, or otherwise improperly accounted for. As Enongo explained:

> [The project is] following those threads, and as part of that, it's recognizing all of the systems that function to make the music industry often a really hostile space for women and girls making music. It's revising the narrative from "we weren't here" to "we were there but it was really fucking hard." And I think that completely shifts common ideas about our creative capacities and about the things we're making and what we're writing against, in a way that points the gaze at the structure as being the problem, and not the artists.

That's the power of an activist historian. In correcting the record or unearthing forgotten truths, they infuse their field with accountability and authenticity, ultimately strengthening it.

THE MULTI-HYPHENATES

In describing her as an activist historian through her work with the-KEEPERS, I've really only given you a sliver of Enongo's résumé. I could also have described her to you as a scholar with a PhD in science and technology studies; as the director of audio at a video-game studio; as an educator who has taught classes including Intro to Rap Songwriting, Rap as Storytelling, and Black Feminist Sonic Practices; or as a DIY rapper who performs and records under the name Sammus.

Portfolio-style careers are not so unusual these days, but I was intrigued by the specific mix of roles Enongo has taken on, because a) she does so many different things within the realm of music (I had never even heard of "ludomusicology" until I met Enongo; turns out it's the study of music in video games, and it's one of her research interests); b) her work also crosses into the realm of movements with her socially conscious rap lyrics and her scholarly treatment of gender issues in music; and c) she's accomplished that rare feat of blending academia with practical endeavors beyond the proverbial ivory tower, which as you know is a special interest of mine. So I asked her how she decided to break with convention to traverse these different realms. Here's what she said:

> I don't want to project backwards and pretend that I had some grand master plan when I really didn't. I think the reason why I pursued both academia and a music career at the same time was in part insecurity and uncertainty about which one to pick. I was also navigating some long-held beliefs about having to pick one. I entered into certain communities where I felt like there were academics who were also wrestling with those questions . . . people who were also similarly having what to me initially felt like a crisis. But having always been in dialogue with folks outside of academia reminded me that I am not beholden to this structure, so I can try to figure something out for myself.

What she learned is that "it's okay to try to do multiple things at the same time," she told me. "It's another option for how to pursue a life."

PATHFINDERS: THE ORCHESTRATORS
AND NEGOTIATORS WHO FACILITATE CHANGE

Speaking of multi-hyphenates, few have been as inspiring to me, or as essential to the global response to climate change, as Christiana Figueres. Born into a family of politicians in Costa Rica (both her father and brother served as the country's president), trained in anthropology and organizational development, and accomplished in both the public and private sectors, she brought all of her skills and experience to bear at the historic United Nations meeting in 2015 that gave birth to the Paris Agreement. If you've heard of the term "net zero" or know that it's important that we reduce carbon emissions enough to keep the Earth from heating by more than 1.5 degrees Celsius, it's very likely because of the global attention drawn to both of these concepts during the high-stakes proceedings in Paris.

The idea that nearly two hundred countries could work together to draft and approve a legally binding international treaty on climate change sounds nearly impossible, but it happened. At the center of these exceedingly tricky negotiations was Christiana, who led the meeting as the executive secretary of the UN Framework Convention on Climate Change.

There are a number of reasons why Christiana was ideal for the role. For starters, having been raised in a developing nation in the Global South, where the consequences of climate change are being felt most acutely, and educated in industrialized countries in the North, which are responsible for an outsize share of the world's carbon emissions, she understood the competing priorities of both hemispheres. Being from a small country was also probably helpful, as larger nations tend to be too important geopolitically to stay neutral on significant policy matters. As a diplomat and the founder of a nongovernmental organization, she had developed leadership skills that were largely independent of positional authority, unlike the South African government minister who was her closest competitor for the role—as Christiana saw it, he represented a more classic, and male, archetype of control. Christiana also speaks three languages, which never hurts in the realm of international relations; and in addition to her life in public service and her NGO experience, she had advised large companies in the private sector, giving her broad exposure to the different types of players whose support would be called upon by the signatory nations.

"Everything that I had experienced and lived and done previously really came together," she told me, reflecting on her appointment to the secretariat. "The universe prepared me."

But if that's what helped her land the position, what were the traits, skills, and approaches that actually allowed her to succeed in it? That's a different question, and it yields a different set of answers—answers that shed light on what it takes to be a great convener who not only unites a group but propels its progress. Because in the end, the formal title she held was no guarantee of success. What allowed her to deliver on the promise of the Paris conference was the role she took on as both a convener and an agitator for progress, or what I would call a "pathfinder."

I think of pathfinders like Christiana as people who invite and elevate dialogue, break stalemates that others might see as hopeless, and smooth the path to putting ambitious goals within reach. In the music industry, this group might include savvy, supportive managers who know how to take an act to the next level, or inventive producers who inspire and coax the best work from an artist. In movements, a pathfinder is a facilitator who can not only get different parties to the table, but help them deliver better results than they ever could have reached on their own.

Christiana would have her work cut out for her in Paris. The previous attempt at a climate treaty of similar scope, at a conference in Copenhagen in 2009, started in disarray and ended in failure. Going into the 2015 talks, it was clear that under Christiana's leadership, climate diplomacy would be taking a different direction. Maybe you'll recognize yourself in one or more of Christiana's descriptions of the traits that influenced her success at the Paris conference:

> I think about myself as a loving thorn in many sides. I wouldn't ever glue myself to the street—that's just not who I am. But I'm grateful to those who do, because that really helps. So I do appreciate being a thorn in people's side, but I don't do it causing pain. That's why I think of myself as a "loving" thorn.
>
> I also brought my conviction that individual wisdom is fine and it's necessary, but it can never match collective wisdom. So the process that we put together was very much based on collective wisdom . . . [and I was] always encouraging people to not just think in their own swim lanes, but also look at the entire pool, at who else is swimming in this direction and, very importantly, who's swimming in the opposite direction and what do they need?
>
> The third piece that was also very helpful is my commitment to Cassandra [from Greek mythology]. That is, I always want to have, in any group discussion, someone whose job it is to find the weakness in whatever is being planned.

Let's make use of that last point not only as an indicator of suitability for the pathfinder role—if you can't handle that kind of conflict or criticism, this might not be the right job for you—but also as a segue to another type of role worth exploring. Spoiler alert: It, too, requires a high degree of comfort with conflict.

CASSANDRA: THE CONSTRUCTIVE CRITIC

In Greek mythology, the god Apollo endowed the Trojan princess Cassandra with the gift of prophecy. But when she refused his overtures, he cursed her to never have her predictions believed. This was too bad for the kingdom of Troy, which might have defended itself better had anyone heeded her prediction about that wooden horse.

As head of the UN's climate secretariat, Christiana had a Russian colleague who always seemed to find the flaws in everyone else's ideas. People were starting to get annoyed. But Christiana saw him as the group's secret weapon. One day she called him and asked if he would formally take up the job of finding the weaknesses or identifying the risks in every proposal brought to the table. Crucially, she informed the rest of the team that she had made this request, effectively reframing his role from that of a bother who would rain on anyone's parade to that of a valuable contributor who could make everyone's work stronger.

Now, this role is a bit different from the others we've explored in this chapter, in that it's not really a job with discrete tasks. An effective Cassandra could arguably hold any role within a movement—it's more about the approach the person takes to testing ideas and voicing criticism than the responsibilities they're assigned (although in the case of Christiana's Russian colleague, what started as a general approach eventually became a formal element of his job). Adam Grant has described these kinds of people as "disagreeable givers," and he happens to think they're vital to any organization that wants to improve.[6] The key thing is, their critiquing comes from a place of genuine caring. The intent is not to rip on others' ideas but to pressure-test the work while pointing out risks and potential blind spots.

A PROBLEM FOR PROGRESSIVES

With the caveat that I don't have much firsthand experience with ultra-conservative movements, it seems to me that progressive movements are especially prone to having their fill of Cassandras. I think this is helpful, for all the same reasons Christiana and Adam Grant see great virtue in nay-saying when it's rooted in good intentions. But I'd be omitting something big if I didn't say I sometimes find disagreeableness, no matter how generous a place it comes from, to be counterproductive and generally maddening. When we know that solar energy is a huge piece of the needed transition away from fossil fuels, it's frustrating to get pushback from environmentalists who complain that solar panels use plastics and take up land and are hard to recycle. It's uncomfortable, too, to have to answer human rights advocates who are rightfully worried about the labor conditions in China, where the bulk of the world's solar panels are produced. All of this debating comes from a good place and touches on a range of issues I genuinely care about. But sometimes I just want solar panels to be solar panels instead of political symbols, and for everyone who wants to reduce the Earth's temperature rise to agree we should install a lot more of them.

I brought this gripe to Adam Grant, to see if my instinct about the level of disagreement within progressive movements—or at least in the climate movement (which in truth crosses the political spectrum but is much more associated with the Left)—made sense to him. "Is this," I asked, "why liberals can't have nice things?"

While we don't have rich data about the personality-trait makeup of the climate movement, Adam hypothesized that climate activism would disproportionately attract disagreeable givers, who are inclined to argue even as they work for the benefit of society. "This is a divisive, contentious space, and you get into it knowing that you have to fight," he noted. "Agreeable people don't like that kind of conflict."

Sure enough, multiple scientific studies have confirmed that while liberalism is linked to compassion and an interest in helping others, liberals on average are less agreeable than conservatives; they don't place the same value on authority or loyalty.[7] In one especially indicative study, researchers analyzed transcripts of church sermons delivered to congregations across the political spectrum, from liberal Unitarians to conservative Southern Baptists, and counted the references to "in-group" concepts. (In social psychology, in-groups are those we feel an affiliation with, like a religious community, a sports fandom, or even a workplace; we tend to favor our in-groups over other groups.) Ironically, clergy on the Left were found to use more phrases related to in-groups, but further analysis showed the intention of those references was mainly to reject, not endorse, in-group values.[8]

I share all of this because if you're trying to play the Cassandra role, or if you're part of a team that's seeking that kind of pressure-testing from a well-intentioned naysayer, it's important to make sure the disagreeableness doesn't end up overshadowing the generosity. Adam Grant offered an important observation about this:

> Having shared tactics is as important for making a coalition
> work as having shared goals. [Sometimes] you run into a
> "narcissism of small differences" problem, where you have

a bunch of people who ostensibly want the same thing, but
have slight divergences in their strongly held views about
how to advance that thing, and so they end up at odds.

In other words, if you completely disagree with the group about the
tactics they plan to take up, this might not be the right place for you
to be a Cassandra.

RIGHT ROLE, RIGHT TIME

Now, let's say your reaction to reading about the Cassandra role
was, "Yep, that's me! That's what I'm good at." How would you
know if you were right about that? Finding a great fit often comes
down to experimenting with different roles—or working with the
rare organization that will proactively evaluate your suitability for a
particular position.

There are plenty of companies claiming to hold the key to se-
lecting job candidates based not on pedigree or past performance,
but on their likelihood of success in the role they're seeking. These
kinds of competency assessments are still used by a pretty slim number of organizations, even in the private sector. But they're all pre-
mised on a similar idea that can be replicated almost anywhere:
Simply list the skills and strengths of people who have already
shown competence in the role, and use it as a rubric to assess other
candidates. Once you have a way to gauge people's skills, you can
then assign or ask them to work on projects in their area of interest
and competence. "Or," Adam told me, "for areas where they're interested but weak, you offer a training program to get them up to the
level of competence that you're looking for." While that makes perfect sense, sometimes I look at the seemingly innate talents of a
skilled messenger and front person like the young climate activist

Greta Thunberg and wonder: Can those of us who harbor dreams of being the next Greta, but lack her considerable talents as a communicator, really expect to be able to train our way into a role like that? Well, yes and no.

"There isn't any skill that you would put in the front-man bucket that isn't learnable," Adam noted. "The question is, given your baseline, can you improve enough to catch somebody who's way ahead? The reality is, there are some skills where the preexisting or natural talent differences are great enough" that even the best training can't fully close the gap.

So it seems Greta's role as the face of the youth climate movement should be safe for quite a while.

THE ACTIVISTS IN THE STREETS

Say the word "activist" out loud and it's likely the people around you will envision someone in a balaclava setting up encampments, marching in the streets, disrupting college graduations, hurling soup at priceless paintings, going on hunger strikes, or even self-immolating (the latter of which, just so we're clear, is not something I would ever, ever encourage). Or maybe they'll think of a specific type of person who would describe themselves as an activist in a grating, self-congratulatory kind of way, when they likely could find much more effective ways to contribute to society than doing whatever it is they claim to be doing. Both of these images are rooted in reality, but neither provides a complete picture of what it means to be an activist.

Let's forget the self-congratulatory types; they usually aren't helpful to the causes they purport to fight for. With the demonstrators in the street, it's a bit more complicated. Yes, their methods are blunt instruments, and their protest signs don't have room for nuance, which makes it easy for critics to dismiss these contributors to societal change as public nuisances with unrealistic demands. But on balance, movements benefit greatly from the passion and public displays of in-the-streets protesters. With their knack for attracting attention to their causes, these demonstrators are crucial in spreading awareness. Although concrete social change often comes down to compromise (as we'll explore further in Chapter Eight), the uncompromising nature of protesters provides an important check on that process, pressuring those negotiating on behalf of the cause to stick as close as they can to the values and mission they represent.

But the in-the-streets protester is an overly narrow concept of what an activist is. Though some might prefer a more anodyne label, like "advocate," arguably anyone working toward social, political, economic, civil, or cultural change is an activist. In that sense, all of the people in the roles we've examined in this chapter could be described as activists—even Bill Nye, who has publicly debated climate-science deniers and routinely urges his fans to vote for political candidates who are ready to address climate change.

There's another important thing that the activists in this chapter have in common: Each came into their role because of circumstance. That's just how life is a lot of the time, but it also reflects the nature of organized social change efforts. Every movement has its own aims or approaches, with unique needs that ebb, flow, and morph. Rather than saddling them with a templated organizational chart filled with predetermined roles, we want movements to have flexibility and creativity in determining the scope of the roles they require.

Front person, trusted messenger, researcher, activist historian, pathfinder, and Cassandra are not actual job titles (well, maybe "researcher" is), but they serve important functions that could benefit just about any organization trying to effect change, in ways that could evolve according to the organization's specific needs. Keep them in mind as you think about ways to plug into movements you care about. And if you still don't have a specific role in mind for yourself, don't stress. In the coming chapters, we're going to look at tactical ideas for building fan bases for movements. It may be that you see a role for yourself in one of those strategies, and that could help to further illuminate things. If that fails, have patience and remember: We all have a stake in society, which means we all have a role in improving it.

A PERSPECTIVE FROM THE FRONT LINES

I've mentioned March for Our Lives a couple of times in this chapter, and thought it might be helpful to share insights from one of its founders, David Hogg, who has occupied multiple roles in social activism. David was just seventeen when he was thrust into the movement world, after surviving the mass shooting at his high school. As a witness to the Parkland tragedy and a preternaturally talented orator with a simple message about gun control, he instantly stepped into the role of trusted messenger, first with television news interviews in the immediate aftermath of the shooting, and then through speeches and lobbying efforts on behalf of March for Our Lives. The student founders of the campaign took on front roles for the broader gun control movement, and for this they were recognized in *Time* magazine's 100 Most Influential People of 2018.[9]

After taking a gap year to focus on the movement and then graduating from Harvard in 2023, David co-founded Leaders We Deserve, a grassroots effort to elect young progressives to Congress and to state legislatures. He spoke with me at his office in Washington, D.C., about his roles and experiences in activism.

You and your classmates who started March for Our Lives together built something from the ground up. How did you know where to start?

We took this awful moment and started directing some of the energy that people had toward a really small goal to start out, which was boycotting sponsors of the NRA. And the reason why that matters is because very few people think of themselves as activists. I don't think I even thought of myself as an activist at the time. But because you give people that small action to do, it starts to build an identity around this group that takes action together, and it gives you a small win to show momentum against a juggernaut of an organization like the NRA.

Then, after you have that win, it's like: Okay, now that we boycotted, or now that you've posted a tweet from your couch, now can you call your member of Congress? And then after that, it's like: Okay, now can you walk out of your school? Basically, you need to start off with low asks that build up. So we went from boycotts to walkouts to showing up in Tallahassee and working to change laws.

Would you say anger has been the biggest motivator for getting things done?

I think it would be right to say that we were incredibly angry and pissed-off after the shooting. But I think there's a better term for it, which would be a sense of righteous indignation at the injustice of what happened. I think anger and righteous indignation can present very similarly.

You know, we're a pissed-off generation. We feel like the country we were taught about when we were growing up is not the country that we were born into at all. I think it's important to note that our generation has really never seen America truly united in any way. The last time that happened was probably after 9/11; it has not happened ever in our lifetimes. The fact that we can't even have safety in our classrooms, where we're learning that democracy is the greatest form of government, and that democracy can't even stop us from getting fucking murdered? It's very angering.

Do you think there are emotions other than anger, like hope, that could be useful in bringing other people into the movement?

I've been hesitant to use hope to some extent, because I think there's a fine line between hope and delusion. And our country has been delusional for a long time.

I see now why we gave people so much hope and inspiration to believe that change is possible, because these kids were standing up. But I also think a certain amount of danger came with it, where older adults got complacent to some extent—not all of them, but there are a lot of people that have come up to me and said, "You know, I'm so glad that you came through here to save us, because my generation just failed you." And like, I want to fucking slap those people in the face because it's so offensive, because it absolves them of the responsibility that they have to do the work to help make things better still, and it puts the onus on us as a generation to address the fucked-up situation that we were born into and had no say over, or vote over, at all.

I think hope is predicated on the chance that something will happen, that it can happen. And I think what our ideology is centered around is believing that it's going to happen. So hope is not something that is required here, because what we're fighting for, it's inevitable. How many moms, dads, sisters, brothers, best friends can you get killed until you have millions of people standing up against you?

So you'll continue in your activism until then?

I guess so. I mean, what else am I going to do? I could have a boring, nine-to-five desk job and just accept what happened to me, or I could spend the one life I have doing something I care about and probably failing—but maybe succeeding.

WAXING LYRICAL

STORYTELLING THAT GOES
BEYOND BUILDING CONNECTION

Most of what I know about music—not playing it, but appreciating it—I learned from my dad. From the Beach Boys to Brandi Carlile, Gary loved artists who could somehow tap straight into his emotions, or transport him to a specific time or place. Even after I grew up and moved out, we continued to do a lot of our exploring of music together. Gary and I always absorbed songs in completely different ways, though. He never focused on the lyrics, at least not at first. Instead, he would take in a song holistically, judging it based not on what it said but on how it made him feel.

I, meanwhile, paid super-close attention to the lyrics from the first listen, and wanted to talk to him about the stories in every song. You could say it was a fixation. But this fixation once helped me tremendously, when I was in college and had failed to do the reading one week for a sociology class called Mistake, Misconduct, Disaster: How Organizations Fail. On a pop quiz, we were asked to describe the management style of Wagner Dodge, the leader of a unit of doomed firefighters in the 1949 Mann Gulch wildfire in Montana. I was caught with my proverbial pants down; I had no idea where Mann Gulch was or what had happened there. But as I reread the question, it dawned on me: This was the story from "Cold Missouri Waters," a folk tune I knew by the Canadian singer-songwriter James Keelaghan. The song is about a ferocious wildfire, and the foreman of a firefighting unit who improvised a clever plan to keep from getting devoured by it. But Dodge failed to get his men to follow his lifesaving instructions. As a result, there were very few survivors of the deadly blaze; he was one of them.[1] In the song, Dodge tells the story from his hospital room (the opening lines are: "My name is Dodge, but then you know that / It's written on the chart there at the foot end of the bed"), recounting the tragedy and his role in it with a level of specificity and emotion that apparently stuck with me. Anyway, I got a 100 percent on the quiz.

WHAT EFFECTIVE STORYTELLING DOES

Educating, persuading, activating: These are major hallmarks of effective storytelling, which can accomplish a lot more than just getting an unprepared college student out of a jam.

Think about the last time you were awed by a speech, outraged by a news story, grabbed by a social media post, or stirred by a piece of music. It took great storytelling to inspire or move you in the moment. But what happened afterward? Were you moved enough to make changes in your life in support of the cause you were hearing or reading about? Did you take action by calling a politician, making a donation, attending a protest, or sharing what you had learned with family or friends? Was your perspective altered, suggesting you had achieved a new level of understanding about the issue at hand? If so, then you likely encountered some truly effective storytelling. If not, then the storyteller only got you part of the way there.

Good storytelling creates an emotional connection with people, which is useful when you're trying to get people interested in a cause. But actually mobilizing your supporters? That's much harder. And that's where effective storytelling comes into play.

Music is filled with models of effective storytelling. We'll examine just a few in this chapter, from artists I admire as much for their societal impact as for their music. We'll analyze different choices they made and storytelling devices they used to communicate their message. We'll consider the role the audience plays in the act of effective storytelling. And we'll meet an incredible leader who unwittingly found herself at the center of a movement, and orchestrated storytelling efforts that have not only won multiple Emmy Awards, but have literally saved lives. Each example underscores the difference between good and effective storytelling.

THE POET AND THE SONGSTRESS

Abel Meeropol was a poet. The son of Jewish immigrants who had escaped the Russian pogroms, he lived a remarkable life in New York City that intersected directly with several key figures and moments in American history. As a high school English teacher in the Bronx, he taught the influential Black writer James Baldwin.[2] Later, he adopted the two sons left behind by Julius and Ethel Rosenberg, the couple who were convicted of spying for the Soviet Union and executed in 1953. Meeropol's early writing was fueled by his family's experience with antisemitism. But the work he is best known for was produced in reaction to the horrors of lynchings in the American South.

On August 7, 1930, two Black men held in a jail in Marion, Indiana, were removed from their cells, beaten by a mob, and hanged from a tree in the courthouse square. Meeropol's poem "Bitter

Fruit" was his emotional response to seeing a photograph of the grisly scene. In 1937, the poem appeared in a New York teachers' union publication.[3] An amateur songwriter and composer, Meeropol also put the words to melody; it was performed a handful of times, including by his wife, Anne.

I'm going to skip ahead a bit to say that if you know the song Meeropol composed, then you know it as "Strange Fruit," which is how it was retitled—and you also know how powerful and searing a composition it is. But the music and lyrics are only part of the story-telling achievement that "Strange Fruit" represents.

In 1939, Meeropol brought his song to Billie Holiday, a Black singer he had seen perform at Café Society, an interracial nightclub in Greenwich Village.[4] The rawness of "Strange Fruit," with "Black bodies swinging in the Southern breeze / Strange fruit hanging from the poplar trees," was remarkable for its time, and still is.

The owner of Café Society made sure Holiday's interpretation of the song reached maximum effect. As David Margolick writes in *Strange Fruit: Billie Holiday, Café Society, and an Early Cry for Civil Rights*, the club owner "decreed elaborate stage directions for each of the three nightly performances. Holiday was to close each set with it. Before she began, all service stopped. Waiters, cashiers, bus-boys were all immobilized. The room went completely dark, save for a pin spot on Holiday's face. When she was finished and the lights went out, she was to walk off the stage, and no matter how thunderous the ovation, she was never to return for a bow."[5]

No "thank you and good night." No encore. Show over. The intention in performing this protest song was to leave people with their discomfort. This was a method of protest in and of itself. Going out for a night of live music at a club is usually associated with having a good time; and good time or not, when people are moved, they generally want to express that to the performer and have their appreciation acknowledged. Holiday did not let her audiences have what they wanted.

Withholding is a tactic used in organizing. It's the core principle behind going on strike. Discomfort, too, can be a powerful motivator. Meeropol was shocked by the photograph he saw, so he wrote a poem about it. Holiday was horrified by the treatment of Black people in the American South, so she sang about it.

Making people feel uncomfortable is a valid choice when you're trying to communicate the urgency of confronting a terrible situation. At the simplest level, people may want to not feel uncomfortable anymore, so maybe they'll do something about it. Perhaps that's what happened when Holiday brought "Strange Fruit" to the executives at her record label. Columbia Records, fearing pushback from radio stations and record retailers in the Southern states especially, refused to make the recording. But they agreed to give Holiday a one-session release from her contract so she could record the song with Commodore Records, an alternative jazz label.[6]

"Strange Fruit" was recorded in April 1939. Radio stations were hesitant to play it. But the record became a huge hit, over time selling a million copies. Upon its release, *New York Post* columnist Samuel Grafton wrote: "It will, even after the tenth hearing, make you blink and hold onto your chair. Even now, as I think of it, the short hair on the back of my neck tightens and I want to hit somebody."[7] The NAACP adopted the song as an anthem for its campaign to eradicate lynchings, which between 1882 and 1964 killed an estimated 3,400 Black people in the United States.[8] Ahmet Ertegun, the legendary Atlantic Records executive who worked with Ray Charles, John Coltrane, and the Rolling Stones, called "Strange Fruit" "a declaration of war" and "the beginning of the Civil Rights Movement."[9]

Sixty years after its recording, in 1999, *Time* magazine crowned it the song of the century. "In this sad, shadowy song about lynching in the South, history's greatest jazz singer comes to terms with history itself," *Time* commented.[10] Holiday was only twenty-three years old when she began performing "Strange Fruit"; she was probably not yet widely considered history's greatest jazz singer at that point. But the song's storytelling power—rooted in the arresting lyrics and mournful melody, but also in Holiday's aching vocals and emotive staging—assured that she would be remembered that way.

Developing effective storytelling isn't easy, but once it's achieved, truly effective storytelling is almost effortlessly memorable.

THE SINGER DOTH PROTEST

Let's fast-forward about twenty-five years from the recording of "Strange Fruit" to the early days of the Vietnam War protests and the competing storytelling styles of Phil Ochs and Bob Dylan. Unless you're well versed in the 1960s American folk music revival, you may not have heard of Phil Ochs. My dad was a big fan and passed his appreciation down to me and my brothers. Ochs (pronounced "Oaks") was a prolific songwriter and activist. He and Dylan played in the same Greenwich Village folk clubs and ran in some of the same circles. But their strikingly different approaches to storytelling put their careers on divergent trajectories.

Ochs studied journalism at Ohio State University,[11] and rarely if ever moved off the newsy, political themes that defined his music. Dylan, meanwhile, quickly branched out from the protest songs that had put him on the map. His plaintive explorations of relationships were wrapped in vague narratives that created an air of mystery around the notoriously reclusive singer while lending his songs wider, and more enduring, resonance. Even Dylan's earlier, overtly political music ("The Lonesome Death of Hattie Carroll" from 1964 is a good example) differed from Ochs's in terms of storytelling technique. Dylan tended to share the facts of a situation and then bring his audience on a journey to a specific conclusion. With Ochs, you started at the end, with his righteous, angry opinions. "Mississippi, find yourself another country to be a part of" went the derisive chorus to "Here's to the State of Mississippi,"[12] in response to the 1964 slaying of three activists during a Black voter registration drive.

Ochs's ripped-from-the-headlines approach directly inspired fans to march for civil rights and demonstrate against the Vietnam War. He also took an active part in protests himself.[13] During the famous unrest outside the 1968 Democratic National Convention in Chicago, Ochs was jailed after a stunt in which he and fellow protesters nominated a pig for president.[14] (Later, he testified that while he went to Chicago to perform his songs at the invitation of protest organizers Jerry Rubin and Abbie Hoffman, he also paid for the pig.)[15] Dylan by then was already several years removed from making straightforward protest music, but his 1963 masterpieces "Blowin' in the Wind" and "Masters of War" and 1964's "The Times They Are a-Changin'" continued to weigh on America's conscience as public opinion began to turn against the war in Vietnam.

The stories artists tell are, at least in part, a product of their times. The number of Billboard Hot 100 singles related to the Vietnam War increased for the remainder of the 1960s, and peaked in 1970 at nineteen.[16] Will we ever again see nearly a fifth of the chart devoted to political music? Today, lyrics that resonate widely are often intimate stories, from songwriters who specialize in dissecting interpersonal relationships (Taylor Swift, Adele, and Billie Eilish and Finneas, to name just a few). With the advent of confessional blogging culture and the social media era that rushed in after it, the rise in popularity of personal narratives about relationships isn't too surprising.

But being an effective storyteller is about more than which stories we choose to tell. It also comes down to how we tell them. Unlike Dylan, who was awarded the 2016 Nobel Prize in Literature for "having created new poetic expressions within the great American song tradition,"[17] Ochs, who died in 1976, never crossed over from the folk scene. His songs had too much invective for that, which limited his overall appeal but perhaps was useful in rallying his core fan base. So who was the more effective storyteller? It all depends. Was Dylan seeking to invent new poetic expressions? Was Ochs more concerned with getting people to protests than attaining Dylan-level fame? Ultimately, the effectiveness of stories is best measured against the specific goals of the storyteller.

Movements, too, face storytelling decisions that can impact the ability to meet a broader goal. Will they use measured language and tell stories that suggest an interest in diplomacy and partnership and broad cooperation? Will they use fiery words and tones to spark action by a potentially smaller but more impassioned group of likeminded thinkers? Will they test humor in a bid to be relatable, fun, or edgy? Every choice holds the possibility of being harmonious—or discordant—with the broader objective.

THE GREAT COMPRESSION

As soon as the 1960s ended, a funny thing started to happen to popular music. The lyrics got far simpler, and increasingly repetitive. That's not me being snobbish just because I love the old stuff. It's something researchers observed in a scientific study of the "compressibility" of songs on the Billboard Hot 100 from 1958 to 2016.[18]

Compressibility is the degree to which a song's lyrics shrink if you take out repeating sections (like the chorus) or repeated multi-word phrases. Arguably, if your lyrics fit into fewer characters of text or bytes of data, and if you use fewer unique words or phrases than songs of similar length, then you have less real estate in which to properly lay out a story, in which case effective storytelling probably becomes more of a challenge.

The researchers surmised that the declining complexity of high-charting pop songs was a function of the increased availability of new music, with listeners drawn mostly to tracks that were easy to remember because of the simplicity or repetition of their lyrics.[19] Sure enough, they found that the compressibility trend kicked into especially high gear after 2006, which aligns nicely with what was happening in the music industry at the time. Spotify was founded in 2006. As it and other digital platforms took hold, song distribution became as easy as uploading a file, setting off an explosion in the availability of music. By 2023, an average of 103,500 new tracks *a day* were arriving on the digital doorstep of the world's streaming services and online music stores. And that was up more than 10 percent just from the previous year.[20]

I suspect we have a window now for complexity to return to pop lyrics. Today, so much music discovery takes place on social media, in snippets. This change was ushered in by TikTok, which became a global force just after the period examined in the compressibility study. If having a sound bite featured on a viral video is enough to drive downloads or streams of the complete track, then it shouldn't matter how complex the rest of the song is, so long as the initial snippet was an earworm. That's how the AJR song "World's Smallest Violin" cracked the Billboard Hot 100 list, which is based on a mix of sales, streams, and radio airplay. The song is ridiculously complex, both musically and lyrically, and my brothers and I had little hope of it being a commercial success—we just really liked it. In

2022, a year after its release, it became one of the top tracks on Tik-Tok. But it wasn't the whole song that went viral. It was just the last twenty-five seconds (the crescendo from "I'll blow up into smithereens" to "So let me play my violin for you"). Next thing we knew, "Violin" made the Billboard Hot 100. Of course, that's just anecdata. It's probably too early to declare an end to the simplicity trend. But it's been clearly demonstrated that in the decades before Tik-Tok, pop music was experiencing a real decline in lyrical complexity.

There's an important takeaway here for movements: Stories are more likely to be shared when they are simple enough to be remembered. But our next example of effective storytelling provides an important addendum: In the right hands, even a complex story can be told (and retold thirty-five years later) in a highly memorable way.

"FAST CAR"

With chart toppers getting simpler after the 1960s, it stands to reason that more complex songs needed to be even better than before to become hits. This was no problem for Tracy Chapman, whose breakout 1988 song "Fast Car" easily cleared the rising bar.

Hopeful. Melancholy. Tender. Resigned. "Fast Car" runs through a range of emotions as it tells the story of a seemingly doomed relationship, from the perspective of the partner who is working hard to escape the confines of her existence. It isn't as blatantly political as "Talkin' Bout a Revolution," which is from the same album, but the character-centered story of "Fast Car" incorporates clear social justice themes about the lives of the working poor and the bleakness of economic immobility. The power of the song rests in part on its catchy hooks—the warm, hypnotic guitar riffs between verses, the melodic, singalong-ready "I-ee-I" of the chorus. But the lyrics are a lesson in effective storytelling all on their own.

What the author and cultural critic Hanif Abdurraqib once re-ferred to as "the miracle of 'Fast Car' " is how it almost impercepti-bly changes who's being addressed at different points of the song.[21] In the first two verses, the protagonist speaks directly to the person she hopes to run off with ("You got a fast car / I got a plan to get us out of here "). There's a sly pivot in the third verse, though, when we learn the character's backstory. Presumably the partner already knows all about the alcoholic father, the mother who walked out, the education cut short by a sense of obligation to the father. The char-acter is relaying her circumstances to us, the listener. Then she turns back once again to the story's antagonist: "You got a fast car / Is it fast enough so we can fly away?" Only this time, we understand her perspective on a much deeper level.

"That is storytelling," Abdurraqib proclaimed in a dissection of the song on a 2021 episode of the podcast *Millennials Are Killing Capitalism*. "That is generous. That's saying, 'You don't know the circumstance, so I'm going to provide you with the tools you need to immerse yourself in it, and then I'm going to turn away from you and let you figure the rest out on your own.' "[22]

Just as withholding is a tool, as Abdurraqib noted, so is "giving people enough scaffolding that they can build the world on their own. And then, even if that world at the end looks a little bit differ-ent than mine, we've still shared the experience of building, which is worthwhile."[23]

"Fast Car" spent twenty-two weeks on the Billboard Hot 100 chart in 1988, peaking at number six. As a reminder of what the song was up against, in the week it peaked, the top song in the United States was George Michael's irrepressibly repetitive "Monkey."[24] The single version of "Monkey" has just 99 unique words spread over the entire length of the track, which clocks in at 4 minutes and 47 seconds, while the single of "Fast Car" contains 187 unique words in just 4 minutes and 26 seconds. (For comparison, Taylor Swift's "Blank Space" has 192 unique words and somehow compresses all of that into just 3 minutes and 52 seconds.)

You may recall that "Fast Car" returned to the Billboard Hot 100 in 2023, peaking this time at number two, after it was covered by country star Luke Combs,[25] who was so faithful to the original that he didn't alter the line "I work in a market as a checkout girl." The fact that the song charted higher in the hands of a white man than in the hands of the Black woman who wrote it triggered an important debate and much-needed introspection by the music industry. But the gorgeous rendition the two singers performed onstage together at the 2024 Grammy Awards seemed to put the controversy to rest. Years after its author had largely left the public spotlight, the evocative storytelling of "Fast Car" had successfully reached a whole new generation of listeners.

There are two important lessons for movements here:

1. Give people the context they need so they can actually make sense of your story, and
2. Simplicity and complexity are not the markers by which we should be measuring effective storytelling.

We should be focused instead on telling stories that are affecting and enduring enough that they can be remembered, and even repeated years later, leaving each new audience as captivated as the people who heard the message the first time around.

WAIT FOR IT

Now let's recall the year 2009—or 1776. Either way, U.S. founding father Alexander Hamilton is about to explode onto the scene.

For the purposes of this chapter, let's stick with the 2009 time frame. In May of that year, celebrated songwriter and actor Lin-Manuel Miranda was invited to a White House "poetry jam." Asked to perform something from his hit musical *In the Heights*, which had opened on Broadway the year before and won four Tony Awards and a Grammy, he instead shared a song from a new project he was working on, explaining: "It's a concept album about the life of someone who embodies hip-hop: Treasury secretary Alexander Hamilton."[26]

By 2012, Miranda determined that his concept album was in fact the nucleus of a new musical.[27] He spent the next few years writing a show containing all the tension, excitement, and tragedy of Ron Chernow's 2004 Hamilton biography, on which it is based. Miranda, however, conveyed the story through hip-hop, R&B, Jamaican dancehall music, and jazz. He also recruited a mostly non-white cast that turned the identities of America's founding fathers on their head, while simultaneously underscoring the stunning lack of diversity elsewhere on Broadway.

Like modern Shakespeare, *Hamilton* brought history alive in a way that civics textbooks, biographies, and the historical record never had. From elementary schoolers on up, Americans were suddenly obsessed with the "forgotten" founding father who wrote the bulk of the Federalist Papers, designed the American banking system, and established the precursor to the U.S. Coast Guard. Miranda's creation received eleven Tony Awards out of an unprecedented sixteen nominations. It took home the 2016 Pulitzer Prize for Drama and the Grammy for best musical theater album. Miranda's father, Luis Miranda—a longtime political strategist, advocacy consultant, and Hispanic community activist—helped broker a unique educational partnership to create *Hamilton*-inspired classroom activities and lesson plans for teachers, along with other digital resources that have reached tens of thousands of students.

So let's use all of that as evidence to declare, uncontroversially, that *Hamilton* is one of the greatest storytelling triumphs of the modern era. Perhaps somewhat more controversially, I would argue that this didn't just come down to Miranda's unique abilities as a playwright and performer, or to the skills of the talented cast and crew working with him. Pardon the heresy, musical theater fans, but we haven't yet discussed the other essential ingredient in effective storytelling: the audience.

Remember that 2009 poetry jam where Miranda first took his Hamilton concept public? Take a look at the YouTube video on the Obama White House channel, which is maintained by the National Archives and Records Administration. The room was clearly supportive of Miranda and appreciative of his lyrical skills, but it responded to the crucial "Alexander Hamilton / His name is Alexander Hamilton" line pretty awkwardly, with only smatterings of bemused laughter. The audience clearly didn't know what to make of it.

Things got way worse the next day on Comedy Central's *The Daily Show with Jon Stewart*. In a segment called "Old Man Stewart Shakes His Fist at White House Poetry Jams," an aggrieved Stewart exclaimed, "You're rapping about Alexander Hamilton?!" The audience laughed at what at first sounded like faux disapproval. "Look, I appreciate you've chosen the pen versus the sword," Stewart said, before slipping into an embarrassing attempt at syncopated rap: "I feel your struggle as you hustle. You've been dissed, disrespected, disenfranchised; but 'dis' is kind of ridiculous . . . because a Black man in a white house, so, you can stop now." More laughs. "Really," Stewart added, seemingly serious in tone as the laughter died out. "You can stop now."[28]

Stewart's reaction to the poetry jam performance is pretty shocking to revisit now. But in May 2009, the gatekeepers of U.S.

popular culture were in no mood for a clever hip-hop retelling of the American Revolution. Less than a decade removed from 9/11 and still mired in a war in Iraq that was entered into under false pretenses, the country was now suffering the acute effects of the worst global financial crisis since the Great Depression.

By the time *Hamilton* arrived on Broadway six years later, though, much had changed. The U.S. economy was back on track and innovation was in the air. Millennials had infiltrated the workplace. Established industries were being turned upside down with the rise of new apps like Uber and Airbnb. America had already elected its first Black president to a second White House term, and the U.S. Supreme Court had just legalized gay marriage. The country wasn't cured, and still isn't, of despair or discrimination. At times it even feels we've traveled backward in this respect. But in 2015, a large portion of the populace clearly embraced the type of progress *Hamilton* represented. Even Jon Stewart, casually chatting with Barack Obama backstage at *The Daily Show* the same month *Hamilton* reached Broadway, said he'd heard the show was "phenomenal."[29] Critics loved it. Audiences, too. And it's not just the history they appreciated. Lyrics like "Immigrants—we get the job done," triumphantly sung by Hamilton and Lafayette, were major applause lines nightly.

America was finally ready for Miranda's masterpiece, which is another key lesson about storytelling: No matter how many times a story is told, it will only be heard and understood if it's communicated to an audience that cares to listen. For movements, that often means telling stories that meet people where they are—but that's not very ambitious. Better yet, tell stories that are powerful, original, and memorable enough to move people along to the next step in their evolution as supporters for your cause. Then you can make them meet you where *you* are.

WHO TELLS YOUR STORY?

One block south of the theater where *Hamilton* found its Broadway home, Brendon Urie made his Broadway debut in 2017, in the musical *Kinky Boots*. The Panic! at the Disco singer earned strong reviews and revived ticket sales for the show, which was then in its fifth year.[30] One night, the fans in the audience included songwriter Sam Hollander.

If you don't know Sam's name, there's still a good chance you're familiar with his work. He has credits on hundreds of tracks, including "HandClap" by Fitz and the Tantrums, "Rock Me" by One Direction, "Someone to You" by Banners, "When You Love Someone" by James TW, and "Ways to Be Wicked" from *Descendants 2*. He also has worked with Carole King, Ringo Starr, Billy Idol, Katy Perry, Blink-182, Gym Class Heroes, and Weezer, among dozens of other artists, and he wrote lyrics for four songs on the 2016 Panic! album *Death of a Bachelor*.

After watching the performance of *Kinky Boots*, Sam went backstage to see its star and noticed a contented but slightly dazed look in his eyes. He was suddenly struck by the singer's impressive career trajectory, from his rise in pop culture to his arrival on the New York stage. It was a lightbulb moment. As Sam recounted:

> At this point, [Brendon] had just hit thirty, and I thought, *What an incredible whirlwind his twenties were.* And that night in the car, I wrote "Roaring 20s" just based on that narrative.

"Roaring 20s" is not Sam's story; it's Brendon's. However, Sam doesn't always tell stories strictly from the point of view of the artists singing his songs. Often the perspective is an amalgamation

forged in the studio during a collaborative writing session, as was
the case with "High Hopes," the five-times Platinum track included
on the same album as "Roaring 20s" (Sam also wrote verses for
"High Hopes"). But sometimes Sam's lyrics really reflect his own
experiences. Take "Impossible Year," the ballad he worked on for
the previous Panic! album:

> Brendon [wanted] something that was lyrically in the tra-
> dition of a standard, but with a sour light on it. I had just
> lost my mom, and my dad was dying, and so "Impossible
> Year" is really about the loss of parents and having very
> little family. I don't know if Brendon could have con-
> nected to that. But I'd like to believe it resonated—loss is
> a very common theme.
>
> I try not to provide any exposition with anybody I
> work with, though, because I think that's suffocating their
> art. So I would never, ever in the creative process intro-
> duce my perspective and what guided it. I think that
> cheapens the art and ruins the ability for the artist to con-
> nect to it, because it really is a shared experience of col-
> laboration. You know, Brendon's changing things and
> tweaking things and adding on, and most importantly, he
> has to sing it. So if I've saddled him with my narrative, it
> might not resonate the same way.

Crafting stories that are designed for other people to tell is tricky
business. Typically, Sam is trying to write lyrics that are completely
authentic to the artist's voice, while also somehow pushing them
into new territory. It usually requires a lot of legwork prior to going
into the studio to collaborate on a song, which is Sam's preferred
way of working:

I spend five days beforehand going down a rabbit hole of social media, of YouTube, of print interviews, and I'm trying to find certain hacks that are going to grant me access to the psyche of the artist. I'm looking for humor, relationships, tone. I'm really just trying to get under the hood and figure out who I'm going to be writing with.

I pitch pretty aggressively. If it doesn't land, I know how to take a step back. But I really am trying to take a step they might not have taken. Even on the One Direction song "Rock Me," I think it was a little sexier in some ways and more overt than some of the stuff they'd been doing previously.

With an artist like Carole King, you know, you're talking about the greatest writer in my lifetime. So to sit with her in a room and really beat up a song together, it's about listening and feeling. Carol is very chordal and very melodic, but she gave space for lyrics. So that gave me room. I just listened to her talk. There were all of these little gateways to her that I noticed, and they all were about positivity and love and uplifting themes. She's an empath, and she's a positive person, with a very positive, activist outlook on the world. And so to write a song called "Love Makes the World" wasn't a stretch.

While each songwriting collaboration tends to have its own alchemy, Sam is always cognizant that a story can be effective, or not, depending on who is telling it. As he put it:

Some [artists] are vessels; some are megaphones. At the end of the day, I have tales bursting inside of me that I

want to get out. And every once in a while I can find an
artist with a similar story to tell.

Though storytelling is often thought of as an individual sport, there
are all kinds of ways for it to become a collaborative process. Abel
Meeropol gave the story of "Strange Fruit" to Billie Holiday, who
then told it in a riveting live performance made all the more potent
by the staging instructions of the nightclub owner. Tracy Chapman
was both the creator and teller of the story in "Fast Car," but it reso-
nated with a whole new audience when Luke Combs arrived decades later and shared the story with country fans, making their
eventual duet at the Grammys an especially powerful moment. And
though Sam Hollander has dabbled in "pitch songs"—writing on
spec for an artist who might take to the lyrics and perform them as
is—he much prefers working songs out with artists who want to
help shape them, as he did with tracks for Panic! at the Disco. The
lesson in each case is that collaboration can heighten the effectiveness of good storytelling.

THE CLIMATE PLOT THICKENS

The conditions for effective storytelling—particularly the audience's readiness to hear a message, and the people they'll be receptive to hearing it from—are things I've been thinking a lot about
since getting involved in climate advocacy, especially after AJR
toured across Europe in the summer of 2023.

When we arrived in Athens in early September of that year,
many of the local businesses had been hastily boarded up. Greece
was used to summer heat waves. It was less accustomed to flash
floods, including one that made its way into our touring team's hotel
rooms several floors up from street level. We drove slowly through

fast-rising waters, hoping we wouldn't be late for our outdoor performance. The cavalcade of umbrellas that greeted us right at the stage was no match for the drenching rains that fell onto us and our equipment. Lightning crisscrossed the sky as we played our songs; we had barely made it through our set when the stadium was evacuated. We were living through the story of climate change—and so were the fans, who were left to clean up the disaster in their home country as we moved on to our next tour stop.

Even the mere threat of intense flooding and other planetary consequences, which climate scientists have been warning about for decades, should have been enough to snap anyone, in any region of the world, to attention. But not long after the concept of global warming entered the public consciousness, the fossil-fuel lobby questioned the science (publicly, at least) and turned it into a political third rail before the climate movement had a chance to find its leading storytellers.

Former U.S. vice president Al Gore is widely credited with reviving the climate movement with his 2006 documentary *An Inconvenient Truth,* in which he provided not only charts and statistics to help people understand climate science, but also a moral and ethical framework for understanding our obligation to act on it. It was effective storytelling for its time.

Today, we can go even further than that. Climate change is quite literally hitting home for people all over the world now. No longer just a far-off threat affecting only polar bears in the Arctic or tiny islands in the Pacific, it has caused devastating fires in California, record-hot temperatures in Texas, a huge uptick in weather disasters across Asia, and those floods AJR encountered in Europe. We no longer need storytellers simply to tell us that climate change is happening. Poll after poll shows that a majority of the public now knows what's at stake; after all, the proof is right outside their windows.[31]

What we still need are powerful storytellers who are not constantly describing disastrous consequences, but sharing stories of a beautiful future, and how we can build it together.

STARTING WITH STORYTELLING

At Sandy Hook Promise, a nonprofit started in the wake of the horrific 2012 school shooting in Newtown, Connecticut, storytelling has been central from the beginning. That's partly because co-founder Nicole Hockley, whose son Dylan was shot to death in his first-grade classroom at Sandy Hook Elementary School, came to the foundation with a strong background in marketing and communications. And partly, the emphasis on storytelling arose because she and co-founder Mark Barden, whose son Daniel was also killed in the 2012 shooting, had no idea how else to channel their grief. So they told, and still tell, stories about their children, carrying photos of their kids with them to speeches, interviews, and Congressional offices, all in the hopes of keeping their children's memories alive and making America's schools safer.

Sandy Hook Promise is focused on teaching people the warning signs that can lead to gun violence. In its first decade of existence, the organization trained more than twenty-one million students, teachers, and parents on how to identify and address potentially troublesome behaviors.[32]

In the same way that it was initially tempting in the climate movement to just let the science do the talking, Hockley said the gun-violence prevention movement is often too focused on data. The numbers certainly are stark. According to the Center for Homeland Defense and Security at the Naval Postgraduate School, the shooting at Sandy Hook Elementary, which killed twenty-six people, was one of twenty gun incidents at K-12 schools in the United States in 2012.[33] That data alone should have been powerful enough to effect change. But clearly it wasn't, because the violence didn't stop—and in fact it worsened in the years that followed. So Hockley doesn't rely exclusively on data to make her plea to fellow parents or to politicians. As she explained it:

> Data is critically important. But each of those numbers is a person, and as survivors or impacted family members, I feel there's a responsibility to bring people back to remembering the person, and you can only do that through storytelling. You have to bring it back to a very individual level and tell that discrete story—and then "macro" it back up. If it's just data, well, no one can see themselves in data, and you can't emotion yourself out of data.

From climate to healthcare to food and now to anti–gun violence, Hockley, a former marketing executive and consultant, has made a career out of getting buy-in from people through storytelling. At Sandy Hook Promise, when she senses she has her audience in the exact right spot to compel them into action, that's when she invokes what she calls "the arc to hope."

> I fully recognize that when I stand up, I am the embodiment of a parent's worst nightmare; people get awkward around me. But I don't want to leave people in that space. I never want to leave someone in a negative place through our storytelling. I want to give them hope for the future, and actions to take to get control back over their environment. You can feel very out of control: "This is so big,

what difference can I make?" Well, it can go into activism, education, or just having a conversation with your kid.

Sandy Hook Promise's public service announcements, made with the help of advertising giant BBDO New York, have helped spread the word about the organization's free programs for schools and its anonymous reporting hotlines. By the end of 2023, the group's hotlines had received more than 185,000 tips, prevented more than five hundred youth suicides, and played a role in stopping at least fifteen planned school shootings that law enforcement considered to be credible threats.[34] Pretty effective, no?

The group's first Emmy for Outstanding Commercial was for "Back-to-School Essentials." This 2019 public service announcement put a modern, macabre twist on typical TV ads for back-to-school shopping, with new sneakers put to work running through a locker-lined hallway to escape an active shooter, and new socks turned into a tourniquet for a student bleeding from a gunshot wound. A second Emmy came in 2022 for a video featuring school shooting survivors singing the lyrics to Katy Perry's "Teenage Dream." The hauntingly written spot was nominated alongside ads for Apple, Chevy, and Meta. And in "Just Joking," a 2023 PSA from the group, comedians—including Rachel Bloom, Margaret Cho, Billy Eichner, Jay Pharoah, and Wanda Sykes—read out actual threats made by real-life school shooters; their audiences mistake the threats for punchlines. Eventually the statements get strange enough that the audiences wonder what's happening.[35]

Here's Hockley again, on how she identifies the moment when stories get their chance to make the leap from "good" to "effective":

> I'm always reading the room while I'm talking. I'm watching people. You can tell when you've captured someone. When they're looking at you—and not just looking,

they're really seeing you and absorbing it—I get a little chill. It's like, *This is landing now.*

It's the same with our PSAs . . . For me, it's still a visceral response, a feeling that I feel in my body. When Wanda Sykes has her line about how "I want to go down as the best school shooter in history," and then looks out at the audience and shakes her head, that's the moment—and I think, *We just got 'em.*

FRESHMAN ENGLISH

This chapter started with a story about a quiz I took in college, so it is only fitting that to wrap up, we go back to the classroom. I had a freshman English seminar where every week we each had to share a piece of our writing. Some weeks it was poetry, some weeks it was essays, other weeks it was short stories. The professor (and sometimes other students) would critique the work. My poetry was particularly ill-received. As painful a memory as this is for me, let's journey back in time there for a brief thought experiment.

Imagine you have to prepare a short story to read in front of the class. The story could be about anything at all. Which storytelling techniques would most appeal to you? Or better yet, which do you think would be most impactful for the audience you are imagining?

WOULD YOU RATHER:

- Build a world and attempt to immerse them in it immediately, or build a narrative that first meets them where they are?

- Tell the story of a problem, or a solution?

- Craft a big story about the world, or a small one about a person, or some combination of the two?

ONCE YOU DECIDED THAT, WOULD YOU:

- Find ways to intentionally make the audience uncomfortable?

- Focus on the simplicity of your message?

- Give your audience tools to make sense of a more complex story?

Very rarely, if ever, can a story do all of these things—and this is far from an exhaustive list of available techniques and storytelling choices. But the same story can be told in thousands of different ways by incorporating various elements from each of these strategies. So have fun with it. Find the versions that resonate most deeply, and that are most likely to educate your listeners or compel them to take some sort of action.

And whether you're continuing on as an English major or working in one of the many disparate fields where great storytelling is needed—journalism, marketing, medicine, law, science, sales, finance, teaching, and technology among them—remember that a good story is not the same as an effective one.

LADDERS AND HURRICANES

TURNING PEOPLE INTO LISTENERS, LISTENERS INTO FANS,
AND FANS INTO MOVEMENT EVANGELISTS

One of the best philosophy courses I took in college was a meta-physics seminar where we spent a lot of time discussing the concepts of individual and group identities. I was already perform-ing with my brothers by then, while simultaneously trying to figure out who I was, as most college students (and adults, it turns out) are prone to do. I was really struggling to reconcile my identity as Adam with my identity as the "A" in AJR. So I paid particular attention in this class, hoping it would resolve some of my bigger concerns in life. It didn't. But I loved exploring the material. Plus, it gave me some important insights into fan bases, which are also just a mix of individual and group identities. I didn't make that connection immediately—fan bases weren't a critical interest of mine at the time, as AJR was still a long way from establishing one—but I started thinking about their dynamics a lot more in the years that followed.

A group, in simple terms, is a collection of individuals with their own identities. But the group itself also has its own distinct identity, which evolves when the experience of being in the collective changes the individual identities that formed the group in the first place. Enough with the abstractions. How about this: The K-pop superfans in the BTS ARMY might be students, or lawyers, or dental hygienists; they might live in South Korea, South America, or South Bend, Indiana; they might relate to BTS in different ways, with some partial to certain songs or band members, while others focus on going to shows, collecting merch, or obsessively tracking the band's every move. But together, these identities of the individual fans help form the singular identity of the BTS ARMY. At the same time, just being part of the BTS ARMY, and being exposed to different influences within the fandom, might change how a person interacts with the songs, experiences the live shows, or relates to others in the community. Then consider that each fan is likely a part of multiple fandoms, and might embody a different identity in each one, thereby differently influencing every fandom they are a part of.

Okay, my philosophy degree is getting the best of me. Let's reel it back in.

BUILDING A FAN BASE FROM SCRATCH

In Chapters One and Two, we focused on finding the movement you want to join and what role you may want to play. Chapter Three armed you with ideas for crafting the message of your movement. But now that you're really in the thick of it, how do you help the movement grow? How do you attract other people to it? How do you build a fan base for it?

In the music industry, a common way of thinking about building a fan base uses the metaphor of a ladder. Fans on the first rung may hear a song in the supermarket and know the melody or a lyric, but might not be able to name the artist. If they go home and listen to it again on Spotify or Apple Music, they move up a rung. They may listen to three or four more tracks and save those songs to their library . . . another rung. They may follow the artist on social media, go to a show, buy a piece of merchandise. Up, up, up.

Underpinning all of this is the music, of course. But in reality, the ladder rests on something even more powerful, which exists far beyond the world of music, and that's the universal desire for belonging, to feel part of something larger than ourselves. The more someone feels this desire, finds something that satisfies it, and wants to share that thing with others, the higher up the ladder they are willing (and able) to go. When AJR started, we had no ladder to speak of, and no record label to help us source one. So we built one, organically, with a lot of help from our earliest fans.

This feels like a good moment to bring in someone who can tell you about AJR's early days with a little more distance from the band than I have. Plus she understands this ladder thing instinctively and won't bore you with a philosophy lecture. It's time for you all to meet Mel.

Melanie Spiegel was raised in Huntington, New York, a bedroom community on Long Island. It's about forty miles from the Manhattan neighborhood where my brothers and I grew up and began performing as AJR. To Mel, journeying into Manhattan as a kid was kind of a big deal, or at least an exciting adventure. When Mel was eight, she and her best friend started buying each other concert tickets at venues around the city for their birthdays. They attended the shows together, a tradition they've kept up for nearly twenty years. Back then, with their parents as chaperones, they would venture out to see artists they had discovered online in the early years of iTunes and YouTube. Mostly they were into boy bands, and the pop idols of the early 2010s. But Mel can tell you about that better than I can. Here she is:

Justin Bieber, Cody Simpson, One Direction—that all
exploded when I was in middle school, so I was prime age
for it. I had my Bieber Fever shirts. I remember getting
my first iPod, and that was huge. Everyone would bring
their iPods to sleepaway camp and share them and say,
"This is what I'm listening to." I had a notebook where I
would write down every song I liked from someone else's
iPod, and when I came home I would beg my mom for
iTunes gift cards.

The first time Mel and her friend climbed a music industry ladder as
concertgoers, they attended a meet-and-greet with Cody Simpson,
an Australian pop singer. Mel's mom went with them. Soon after
that, the British singer Conor Maynard came to town. A fan account
on social media posted that he would be somewhere in New York
City on a specific day at a specific time, dropping further hints
throughout the week of his arrival. Mel and other fans breathlessly
awaited news of where to find him. The hunt for Conor eventually
led fans to Dylan's Candy Bar, a store on the Upper East Side of
Manhattan. Mel begged her father to leave his office early that day to
take her there. He agreed, and Mel got a glimpse of her idol—while
her lawyer dad, in a suit and on his BlackBerry, was misidentified by
kids in the crowd as being Conor's manager and the architect of the
fan-hunt campaign. (He's still happy to claim he was the master-
mind of all that, by the way.)

In 2013, AJR opened for the Wanted, a British boy band à la One
Direction, at Roseland Ballroom on West Fifty-second Street. Mel,
who was sixteen by then, didn't plan on enjoying the show. The
Wanted was her best friend's obsession, not hers. It was pouring
rain that evening, and she tried to convince her friend to stay home.
But they went. They got there just in time for the first opening act, a

band that was severely lacking experience playing for Roseland Ballroom–sized crowds. I'll let her tell you what happened next.

We showed up as AJR got onstage. They were the first opener of two, and they just immediately won me over. They walked onstage with three white buckets they used as drums, and a stand that Jack clearly stole* from his high school, to put their equipment on—I mean, it looked like a choir stand they took from the chorus room. It was so awkward, but endearing. They plugged in their equipment; there were definitely no roadies with them. They walked off the stage—and then they walked back onstage twenty seconds later, like, "Hey, you didn't just see that." And I remember thinking, *That's kind of cool and interesting*. They were literally just three boys onstage with bucket drums, and I thought that was so fun.

After the concert was over, they were outside the venue while the second opener was doing a meet-and-greet. They were carrying all of their stuff, basically just walking to the subway, and fans started running up to them. After that, I saw them open for Fifth Harmony, and then they did their own show, where there were maybe twenty people max. You could just see it, though. It was like, *There is something here I want to be a part of.*

The next time Mel saw us was at a radio station near her hometown. Back in 2014, when AJR was releasing its first real single and Tik-Tok was still a few years away from being invented, turning a song

---

*Okay, in Jack's defense, I can truthfully say he did not steal that music stand; we had very little money back then for equipment, and I distinctly remember us searching for and buying the cheapest stand we could find. But given the amateur vibe of the whole setup, I forgive Mel for suspecting it was lifted from the choir room. And I wish we had thought of doing that.

into a hit meant it had to be played on the radio. So we got a minivan and drove across the country to play acoustic songs for radio stations. Sometimes this happened at the station itself; sometimes it happened in a bowling alley, at a Buffalo Wild Wings, or at a trampoline park—wherever the local station might be showing up for an event in the community. That initial road trip took us to Ohio, Missouri, Texas, and beyond. But our very first stop was much closer to home. When we turned up at WBLI, a radio station on Long Island, we were pretty unsure what to expect from our first adventure in radio promotion, but we definitely weren't expecting Mel. When we noticed a teenager sitting with her mom in the lobby, a member of the station staff told us the girl was a fan who had heard the DJ announce a short time earlier that we would be stopping by, and she just showed up. To see us.

We were going to need a taller ladder.

EVERY MOVEMENT NEEDS A MEL

BTS has the aforementioned ARMY, Taylor has her Swifties, Harry has the Stylers. All of these legions started with a core group of devoted fans who quickly scaled the ladder of engagement. Presumably, each of them had a Mel.

Our Mel saw our fledgling band as a secret that she was determined to share with the world. She was especially active on our Facebook fan page, where she was constantly suggesting ideas to help get the word out about AJR and getting to know other fans in the group. This would serve her, and especially us, extremely well in the years ahead.

When AJR was on tour in the fall of 2014, Mel was starting college in upstate New York. A double major in anthropology and film studies, she was certain early on that she wanted a career in the entertainment and live events business. As a freshman, she told her parents there was just one gift she wanted for her birthday that year: a rented bus for the evening, so that she could bring a big group of friends from school with her on the hour-long trip to an AJR show in Syracuse, New York. Mel didn't know until she got there that the band was so small at that point that the show was in the basement of a strip club on the side of a highway. After the concert, Mel's friends, at least a few of whom we could now count as fans, took her to a birthday dinner at Chipotle. By the end of that school year, she was an official volunteer member of the AJR "street team," which helped to spread the good word organically through online groups and fan meetups.

Online, Mel continued to be an evangelizing presence for us. But something else was happening, too. She was turning our fan page into a community, where she engaged other fans, who in turn engaged others, in conversations about their lives, their achievements and failures, their frustrations about school or work, their excitement over winning a soccer game or the science fair.

If you're familiar with AJR, then you know we sing about a lot of things other bands typically don't, like going to therapy, or feeling anxious about adulting, or worrying if we can follow up one success with another. In those early years especially, when our fans were depressed from a breakup, they would come to the community to discuss "Turning Out," a ballad about not understanding love. When they were pumped, they listened to "Burn the House Down," about organizing for change. When they were commiserating, they listened to "100 Bad Days" (encouraged, I hope, by the rest of the line: "makes 100 good stories"). Our music validated their feelings and provided antidotes to their emotional crises. In less dramatic moments, our songs about growing up and figuring out yourself and your position within your friend group provided a soundtrack to their everyday lives. These fans discussed all of it—the music, the crises, the quotidian details of their existence—online, with one another. And Mel responded to them, or at least ensured that someone from the extremely decentralized power base of our various fan channels did.

Often, fans from the online community would show up at our meet-and-greets. Mel would usually let us know in advance if there were some important facts we should know about them—maybe they were celebrating their graduation from high school or attending their tenth AJR concert—so that when we met them, we could acknowledge their milestones. This often goes a long way with fans. But it's not lost on me that besides meeting us and snapping a selfie, and in addition to enjoying the music during the show, our fans are often there to see one another. Concerts are a big meetup opportunity for a community that's mainly virtual. Even in the absence of a physical gathering, though, this is a community with very strong ties. Just listen to what Mel says about that:

> The fans are very nurturing and protective of each other. They connect with the songs for a reason. Many of AJR's songs are about mental health or depression. And I think because of the connections the fans have to the music, it allows for deeper connections to be made between themselves. It's very genuine. Because they're not the biggest band in the world yet, it's very much like, "This is my band, I want to watch them grow." But then there's a community that's already established, and they want to join into that, too. So I think a lot of people come for the music and then stay for the community, because once you're a part of it, I think the AJR fans in particular are

very warm. It's like their secret they want to share, but only with people who are passionate, too. The fans want to go to concerts, they want new releases. But in between the cycles of albums, they want to be online, they want to dissect everything that's happening, they look for Easter eggs, and they want to connect.

And really, this is the incredible thing about a strong fandom. The artists in one sense are at the center of it, but we're not *really* at the center. We're a distant entity that makes people feel something through music. But other fans? They are accessible. They engage online, chat about their day, make and share fan art. You could recognize a kindred spirit in this group. You could be their friend. You could even marry them. (That's not a joke; we know of multiple couples who met online through AJR fan communities, lived in different parts of the world, and ended up getting married because our music brought them together.) The fan experience becomes part of the fan's identity.

EVERYONE IN THE FAN BASE OWNS PART OF YOUR SUCCESS

In the music industry, word of mouth might get people to grasp on to the lower rungs of the ladder, but this is much more effective when it involves the right words coming from the right mouths (much like in storytelling). Even once people are intrigued, though, it's easy for them to slip into apathy: *Eh, I'm just having a look around; someone else is going to do the actual work that's needed.* No. You are. But you are only going to do it if you're made to feel important, maybe even invaluable. And that's exactly the sense Mel gave to new fans as they joined the AJR community. She recalls:

I had spreadsheets of all these fans with all their email addresses. At concerts I'd go around to everyone at the meet-and-greet, first with a notepad and then with an iPad. The cost of the meet-and-greet was giving me your email so we could put you on the mailing list for when the band was back in town. I'd engage with the really big fans and mail them stuff so they could mail it out to their friends—so they could be me, but not in upstate New York. They're in Philly, they're in D.C., in rural Pennsylvania, in Florida. I'd send packages of stickers to them to send out to their friends; I'd mail fifty posters to one fan and tell them to put these around your town and send them to your friends. I mean, you're just not going to get a more supportive person than a teenage girl who has a mission on her mind. It's a go-to-the-ends-of-the-Earth kind of thing. I'm outsourcing to the major fans I know I can trust. In return, I make sure to listen to them about what they want to do, and why, and present it back to the band.

FROM LADDERS TO HURRICANES

In a sense, our fan base started growing not from the ground up, but from the inside out. So let's set aside the ladder for a minute. The new people you're reaching are the ones who need the most attention. Bring them into the fold (or have a Mel who can do that for you), hold them close, teach them the ways, and then send them out into the world to do the work, change minds, and send others back in, creating an even bigger community. My visual for this isn't a ladder but a powerful weather system, a hurricane that sucks people in and pushes them back out as it rotates and rumbles along. To be clear, the ladder is how fans engage when they have already committed to the fan base. The hurricane is how we engage new fans. This circular model doesn't work in a vacuum, though. If there is nothing to engage new fans—no new albums, tours, or merchandise to draw people in—the hurricane gets downgraded and continues to weaken.

Mel didn't approach us with a blueprint for a hurricane. What she has always understood instinctively, though, is that fans need to feel like their voices are heard, that their actions to spread the music are making a difference, and that collectively, the whole operation is working and growing. Once they become part-owners, the success is (partly) put on their shoulders.

Mel and the fans she engaged with considered it their responsibility to make AJR into something bigger. To do that, one Mel needed to become ten Mels, and then a hundred Mels, and then a thousand Mels, which is exactly what Mel accomplished. She did it by incentivizing participation and building a strongly bonded community of sharers, without ever making herself the face of the fan base. Instead, like an early investor diluted by those who pile in after at a higher valuation, she gave away ownership of her movement to make room for thousands of other owners. After several years of minding the AJR fan page on Facebook, she ceded it to a young woman from the United Kingdom. When that fan stepped up, Mel didn't mind one bit. Or, as she tells it, "She kind of just took it over one day, when the band was coming to the U.K., and she's awesome."

Meanwhile, another fan, in Boston, grabbed the reins of the main AJR fan account on Twitter (and even met her fiancé through it). As a result of the transfer of responsibilities, the posts on that account started to feature a voice of their own, distinct from Mel's. As with the British fan who had taken over the Facebook page, Mel didn't mind. Her attitude was that both of these fans—and many others who have volunteered their time and passion on AJR's behalf—had shown themselves perfectly capable of handling the job and in fact brought something else of value to it. Meanwhile, the new diehards still respected Mel as the original Mel, while also feeling a sense of equality among all the Mels.

As for AJR? We found some fun ways to connect with fans directly, and to connect fans with one another, which I'll delve into more in Chapter Six. But mainly, we just kept giving the Mels the tools (the music, the videos, the shows, the merchandise, and, maybe most important, the space) to bring other people into the movement. By most metrics it was the exact right strategy. Over the years and on several occasions, we tried to take a more typical industry approach and grow AJR's fan base just for the sake of growing it. We hopped on trends, posted about pre-save campaigns for forthcoming singles, and inundated fans with advertising. It rarely worked for us. We were always better served by empowering the people who got us to this point to do the thing that they wanted: to own a piece of our success. Sometimes I'll see devoted fans post online about how they wish we were still their little secret. (Sorry! That's your fault just as much as ours . . . but also, thank you.)

Collectively, the people either clinging to or climbing up different rungs of the engagement ladder are what you would call a fan base. But a fan base is way more than an aggregation of individual fans. You can easily sense this when the audience sings together at a concert, or when debates erupt in the comments section on a fan-created YouTube channel. A fan base is a community, one that both generates and fulfills the desire for belonging, one that's capable of both acting and inspiring others to act (more on this in Chapter Seven).

As Mel brought more people in to start climbing the ladder of engagement with AJR, she climbed her own career ladder, too, going from fan to superfan to street team member, to street team leader, to digital strategist, to head of fan engagement, to essentially AJR's chief listening officer. It became an actual, paying job for her—but it certainly wasn't in the beginning, or in many of the years that followed, when she supported us through volunteer efforts rooted simply in her passion for the music and her belief in us. Mel is what every movement needs: a champion, a die-hard activist, a fan at the top of the ladder, an orchestrator of hurricanes. Okay, let's put some Mel-ness into some movements.

WHY MOVEMENTS NEED FAN BASES

At social change organizations, the approach to finding and mobilizing supporters runs the gamut from the highly disorganized to the extremely well-honed. Either way, few change agents would argue these efforts have been sufficient. Forget the long-term goal of creating hurricanes that continuously fuel themselves and increase in strength. Progressive movements have lost key ground since the mid-2010s, with their supporters only able to watch as the U.S. Supreme Court stripped away federal protections for abortion, or as energy giants won rights to develop more oil fields. Movements clearly need more commitment from more supporters—arguably always, but especially now. Incidentally, a public with much to be angry about could turn out to be helpful to organizers. Emotions— even a negative one like anger—can be potent forces for social change. But research by Monique Mitchell Turner, from Michigan State University, suggests moral anger is far more helpful to movements when it is paired with the belief that something can be done about it.[1] By validating the anger and steering it constructively, social change organizations provide like-minded people with something to cling to. And that something just might be the lowest rung on our proverbial ladder.

Beyond just amassing supporters, a fan-based approach to movement-building provides another important ingredient for successful campaigns: creativity. As you bring in more people, you'll find them identifying with the movement's tactics and even its goals in somewhat different ways than the people who joined up before them. That's the essence of diversity, which has a well-documented effect of enhancing the creativity of teams and the individuals who comprise them (think about the roles from Chapter Two). And the incredible thing about having a creative fan base is that it engages other fans! When Mel was still in college, we gave her a large overstock of AJR T-shirts we found in a storage unit, all size extra-small. We normally have a pretty even distribution of sizes for our merchandise, but these shirts were comically tiny. We knew hardly anyone who could fit into them. Mel took them off our hands and decided to use them for crafts. She did an Instagram Live showing how to turn concert shirts into pillowcases, solving the problem of our extra inventory while creating yet another opportunity to engage with fans.

Social media has given musicians unprecedented insight into the creativity of their fan bases, thanks to "user-generated content," or UGC. That's digital-marketing-speak for social media posts made by normal people, and not by brands that happen to be in the mix. And this stuff is amazing. Seriously, no matter how many times AJR might have posted about new songs we've put out, none became a hit without the multiplier effect of UGC. Take "World's Smallest Violin," released in 2021. For all the love and attention AJR gave it on our own social media accounts, the song didn't go viral until the following year, and only after a small group of anime artists started putting it in TikTok videos showing the progression in their drawing skills.[2] As the music speeds up to the final crescendo ("I'll blow up into smithereens and spew my tiny symphony . . ."), each subsequent artwork flashes by, faster and faster. It's a clever concept I wish we had thought of—only I'm certain it wouldn't have taken the song as far if we had posted it ourselves.

Soon after the anime artists started using the song in their videos, other people borrowed the idea to show the progression in their own work, and things exploded from there. It was similar with "The Good Part," a track we released in 2017 and which had hardly any streams until a Brazilian athlete used it in a video showcasing her Olympic trials performance, and then cutting to her at the 2020 Olympic Games themselves—or so we heard. Despite many attempts, I've yet to pinpoint the original post that started the trend. But I can confirm that the song only became a hit, years after its release, thanks to social media. Inspired by the people sharing posts that featured our song, we started posting our own version of these videos, with the same track playing in the background. And we can get more meta from there. When our fans post about us or create videos featuring our music, and we make reaction videos or TikTok duets in response, we're interacting with content in which fans are interacting with us or our music, further feeding the fan base.

A terrific parallel to all of this in the movement world is the ALS Ice Bucket Challenge, which raised $115 million for the ALS Association in just six weeks, and increased its annual funding for ALS research globally by 187%.[3] It was the organizational equivalent of life-changing money. But the Ice Bucket Challenge wasn't actually started by the ALS Association; the challenge didn't even have anything to do with ALS, initially. It was simply a fun way for friends to goad other friends into making donations to whatever charity they wished. According to *Time* magazine, that all changed in the summer of 2014 when a friendly challenge was put to a golfer named

Chris Kennedy, from Sarasota, Florida, by someone who had donated to a local child's cancer care fund. Kennedy chose to support
ALS research in honor of a family member with the disease, and
challenged a relative, who picked the same cause.[4] The idea, quickly
branded the ALS Ice Bucket Challenge, went viral soon after. The
ALS Association, suddenly flush with funding for research, went on
to encourage supporters to sign up for a "CEO Soak," a corporate
fundraiser idea inspired by the Ice Bucket Challenge.[5] Awareness of
the CEO Soak isn't even close to the familiarity people have with
the Ice Bucket Challenge, but it's a fundraising tool the association
didn't have until the fan base led the way.

It all goes to show, a movement can learn a lot from its fans, just
as fans can learn from the movement. The more the fans learn, the
likelier they are to move up the ladder. And the more the movement
learns, the likelier it is to reach more fans.

HOW MANY FANS DO MOVEMENTS NEED?

Building effective movements isn't just a numbers game, although
there is research suggesting the existence of a tipping point at which
enough of the population demonstrates support for social change
that it actually happens. Harvard political scientist Erica Chenoweth
calls it "the 3.5% rule." Researchers collected data on more than 300
instances of civil resistance from 1900 to 2006. In addition to finding
that nonviolent campaigns had double the success rate of violent
ones (political change resulted 53% of the time when the action was
nonviolent, versus 26% for violent measures), in a BBC article,
Chenoweth observed that none of the campaigns failed once 3.5% of
the affected population participated in a peak event (such as a mass
protest).[6]

The 3.5% rule has since been adopted by movements including the activist group Extinction Rebellion, which uses civil disobedience to draw attention to climate change. Whether that's the right target is up for debate. As critics have noted, securing greater responsiveness to climate change in a liberal democracy involves a much different set of conditions than campaigns against autocratic governments or occupying military powers, which are mainly the types of campaigns Chenoweth and others studied.[7] But suffice it to say, there are few social activist groups that, presented with an opportunity to grow their support base, would say, "No thanks, we've got enough."

A WORD OF CAUTION

It's hard to be a fan of a cause. Climate action, gun control, women's rights—these are broad concepts involving movements within movements. In that sense, causes are sort of like K-pop. You might really like listening to K-pop, but there aren't many opportunities to show fan support for the genre broadly; if you're wearing a T-shirt reflecting your interest in the music, it's going to be a shirt for a specific band, not for K-pop in general.

So, in the world of movement-building, whether you're setting up the ladder or hoping to fuel a hurricane, it's helpful to be able to connect people to something tangible, such as an issue in their own community that speaks to the larger cause. The problem with local issues is that they tend to get technical very quickly. For example, when the broad goal of climate action is translated into something more specific—say, municipal rules on water usage or farming subsidies at the state level—the motivation that comes from potentially being able to make a direct, local impact tends to be offset at least in part by the inscrutability of the solutions. The math underlying a particular cost or tax may be complicated, and the language of the proposals themselves is probably dense with confusing legalese.

It's also important to note that the ladder model is imperfect for movements where there are real limits on the impact of individual action, as is the case with climate action. There are two reasons for this. First, often when people take an initial small step, like switching to a reusable water bottle, they tend to feel they've done their part. They don't continue up the ladder because they don't see a direct or immediate impact from their action, the way they would if they had bought a ticket to see a new band they've gotten into, with the visceral, instant benefit of enjoying the concert experience. The other big limitation is that ladders are built for individual action, when what's really needed to solve a problem as big as climate change is collective action. So we need to be thinking harder about how to engage people on this particular issue.

But don't despair! Our hurricane model is still very relevant here. As the climate movement attracts more scientists, engineers, farmers, lawyers, artists, politicians, and corporate types, and sends each of them back out to recruit their colleagues or followers to join the cause, knowledge and influence gather like the converging winds of a hurricane, strengthening the movement and propelling it forward.

HURRICANE PREPAREDNESS

The cause that's most important to you is likely advocating for changes you care about. And one of the ways you can help is by advocating for the cause. To do this effectively, start by asking yourself these questions:

- Who do I want to see joining me in the cause?

- Where will I connect with them?

- What message will connect with them?

- Which tools or materials do I need to get that message across?

- When they show interest, what is the follow-up ask or suggestion that will move them up the ladder of engagement with the cause?

- How can I best prepare them to then bring their own friends/family/neighbors/colleagues into the cause?

Need more ideas for completing this exercise? Read on. The next several chapters explore a range of tactics for connecting with people and—the real secret to growing fan bases—connecting people to one another.

HAMMERS AND STRINGS

OPEN THE LID ON YOUR PROCESS AND
REVEAL THE INNER WORKINGS

rowing up, my brothers and I were obsessed with Peter Jackson's Lord of the Rings trilogy. Over and over, we watched the extended-version, four-disc DVD sets for each film. As much as we liked the movies, we especially liked watching the two discs per set containing behind-the-scenes footage. How the set miniatures got built, how the actors got blue-screened into their incredible environments, how the crew could create a scene showing 10,000 Orcs running through Middle-earth—we wanted to know *everything*.

None of us have parlayed this deep interest into a career in film production yet, though Jack and Ryan both studied film for a time in college. The reason I mention LOTR is that, like a lot of people, when the three of us find something we love, we're often just as interested in how it got made as we are in the thing itself.

It was Ryan who realized how we could incorporate this idea into AJR's performances. From our earliest headline touring dates, he began giving concert audiences a peek at the songwriting and production process. During these "making of" segments, he explains the different elements that come together to create a particular track. Even fans who don't much care about music production get interested, probably because Ryan designs these segments to engage people's eyes and ears, but also because he never immediately reveals which track is being broken down. That's a maneuver he learned from one of our favorite artists: the Beach Boys (our parents raised us on them). Early in our music career, Ryan saw some old footage of the band, from when they were still early in their own careers. He vividly remembers watching lead singer Mike Love briefly explain the different musical inputs that went into the making of one of their more popular songs, without giving away the title. It would have been perfectly reasonable for Ryan to stay fixated on the band when the suspense was over and the song was finally revealed. But the musicians were not the people he was focused on. I'll let Ryan explain:

> As soon as everyone figured out what song it was, I saw the audience reaction. It was like, "You just did a magic trick in front of me—I didn't even see what was coming." I thought we could do that and bring it into the twenty-first century. Now it's probably the most successful staple of our show.

Ryan is biased, of course. But he's not wrong. Having participated in these segments over multiple tours now, I suspect their popularity is rooted in the same dynamic that made us so interested in the behind-the-scenes footage from The Lord of the Rings—only it's heightened by the sense of buildup we create, over a much longer segment than that old Beach Boys song reveal.

Ryan always starts these segments with an AJR song's origin— usually he describes a sound he was inspired by, like a knock at the door or a set of keys dropping. Then he has us demonstrate an early iteration of the music. He begins with a beat, layers in different kinds of drums, asks us to bring in a bass line and horns; then he speeds everything up or slows it all down, and instructs us to try out different chorus melodies. Without ever getting pedantic about it, he introduces a handful of important concepts in producing and writing, like swing versus straight beats, or the difference between 3/4 and 4/4 time signatures. The audience follows the transformation of the music with their ears, of course, but also their eyes, as we display on big screens behind us the specific notes or changes in waveforms that map to what they're hearing. Ryan has a condition called synesthesia, which is a blending of the senses and the way in which sensory information gets routed through the brain. It's not harmful, but it is unusual. People with synesthesia might see sounds, hear shapes, or taste words.[1] When Ryan listens to a sound or a song, he often sees a shape or color. Maybe this has made him especially well-suited to bring our music-making process to life on a concert stage, where we can indulge our craving, and the audience's, for a multisensory experience.

Finally, at the segment's conclusion, we arrive at the sounds and tempos that give the track in question its most distinguishing properties. The audience suddenly recognizes it and squirms with excitement as we segue into our performance of the track in full. Ryan refers to this as the moment when the song "explodes," and it's basically what he lives for as a performer.

But even Ryan will tell you it's not just the anticipation that makes the "making of" moments so engaging. Hundreds of thousands of people have watched his "breaking down the production" videos on YouTube, where Ryan offers much more in-depth tutorials. The title of the specific track he's breaking down is listed right in the name of the video, and people still click in and follow along as he explains various elements of the song, takes live questions, and shares his laptop screen to show the specific Pro Tools settings he used to create our sound. What he's doing is giving fans a look at the inner workings of what we do, in effect lifting the lid off the proverbial piano to show all the hammers and strings hidden inside.

Pro Tools, which debuted in 1991 and inspired a wave of competitors like GarageBand, Logic, and Ableton, allowed musicians at any level to record digitally instead of on old-fashioned tape; the software pioneered a way to visualize the digital recording on a screen, whether in a studio or on a home computer. A complete democratization of music soon followed, meaning that musicians could make quality recordings even without having access to expensive studios.[2] In *The Beatles: Get Back*, Peter Jackson's extremely behind-the-scenes documentary about the making of the Beatles' 1970 album *Let It Be*, there's absolutely no indication that any aspect of this miraculous album could have been replicated outside the confines of an old-school studio—because in 1970, it couldn't have been. But AJR fans watching Ryan's production breakdowns of our songs can follow along right from their couches or bedrooms, on their own laptops with their own digital audio workstations, where they can use the same tools, functions, and digital instruments that helped us create our sound. There is nothing Ryan does to make or manipulate songs that you can't see on the graphic interface he shares. What you can't see, however, is the point of view that serves as the starting point for all of our music. For us, that's the artistry, and the place that our sound (in the singular) actually comes from. And that's not something Ryan tries to teach—because it's AJR's, and because we would rather see other musicians develop their own points of view, and also because we wouldn't know how to teach this part even if we wanted to. But the literal sounds (plural) that add up to a song? Ryan will gladly explain those, and show you different ways to morph them, and you are welcome to play around with them however you choose.

I'm not aware of other contemporary bands with our reach who regularly provide an insider's view of the music production process to this extent. But Ed Sheeran has been known to show concert audiences and his social media followers how he builds his sound with a loop pedal, recording and then repeating drum sounds, vocals, a bass line, and other elements that essentially turn him and his acoustic guitar into a one-man band. And there are plenty of other ways in which artists peel back the curtain on other aspects of their work. Questlove wrote at length about his creative process in the book *Creative Quest,* for example, while producer Mark Ronson helmed an insider-y Apple TV+ series called *Watch the Sound,* about different technologies used in music studios. Other performers have shared more personal takes on their lives as musicians, in many cases pushing the boundaries of what's fair game for audiences to see— like Selena Gomez did in *My Mind & Me,* a documentary that searingly put the spotlight on mental health issues and other challenges she faced during a six-year period captured by the cameras.

Why do we musicians open the hood and let people look inside for a sense of who we really are and how we do what we do? And how does any of this relate to movement-building?

WHY WE DOCUMENT

There are lots of ways in which AJR gives fans a glimpse of how we do what we do. In addition to Ryan's song production breakdowns, we put out tour documentaries, post candid moments on social media, and give lengthy interviews. We do all this for many reasons, but mainly because fans like it, and because opening our process to them deepens their connection to our work—much in the same way that the DVD extras intensified the interest my brothers and I had in the Lord of the Rings movies. Watching the behind-the-scenes material made us feel like insiders who understood more than the average person watching the films; it wasn't a sense of ownership, exactly, but somehow it raised the stakes for us and increased our appreciation for the work.

There's another reason we share the process as much as we do, and that's for posterity's sake—which isn't as egotistical as it sounds. For every major headline tour we've done, we've produced a documentary, each made up of several episodes running for as long as twenty-five minutes apiece, showing how our concerts come together behind the scenes. We watch these tour docs every few years, often with our road crew. It helps us to see how we've grown and reveals any aspects of our live performance and tour operations that still need improvement. It also allows newer fans to see what we were like before they discovered us, so that their understanding of the band doesn't have to begin with us as we were on the day they first learned about our music.

Watching the tour docs, you might see us working with production designers or magicians, or tag along with me on a day trip to give a speech to young climate activists. There's also a lot of downtime on tour, and you'll see some of that, too, in scenes of us backstage joking around or coming up with ridiculous contests with our crew to pass the time. And then there are the unforeseen moments of drama, like the show when we needed to make changes on the fly after the giant video wall on stage stopped working, or the night Jack needed to go to the hospital to get treated for losing his voice, or the scary moment during a performance in Salt Lake City when a girl in the audience had a seizure.

Onstage, separate from the microphones that blare our voices and instruments into the arena, we have a set of "talkback" microphones that allow us to talk only amongst ourselves and our crew, which is useful when things go awry onstage or we want to make last-minute changes to the show we've rehearsed. We're always recording what's happening in the talkbacks (again for that opportunity to evaluate and hopefully improve on our responses to problems), and often we'll put that audio into the tour docs, which is about as unique a vantage point as we can give to anyone who wasn't actually up on the stage with us.

Providing a behind-the-scenes perspective is also helpful to movements, for all the same reasons:

- It deepens relationships with supporters

- It creates a chance for teams to review and appreciate their progress

- It gives newcomers a chance to learn more about the history of the movement

- It provides an insider's view that can increase appreciation for the work

Of course, some movements already do this quite well. But it does require a few conceits. First, any stumbles in the process (and who doesn't have those?) require a willingness to explain what didn't work, so that audiences can fully appreciate the aha moments that lead to success. The packaging of AJR's production breakdowns and tour docs is intentionally digestible, yes, but it's also pretty unvarnished. We don't shy away from showing things that went wrong (a decision to cancel the first stop on our 2024 tour for *The Maybe Man* because of a show production snafu was a deep sting for us, and it was all documented by our videographer), and we don't try to pretend that our best work or biggest hits emerged in perfect form. Ryan will tell you on the production breakdown video for "Weak" that the original chorus to the song was:

> *But I'm weak,*
> *and I fell for that.*
> *Boy, oh boy, I should have stayed away from that.*[3]

It was our manager, Steve Greenberg, who pushed us to come up with something more anthemic—something that had an actual point to make. And so we changed the lyric to:

> *But I'm weak,*
> *and what's wrong with that?*
> *Boy, oh boy, I love it when I fall for that.*

When Ryan plays the original demo versus the finished product, and explains how this tiny tweak in the language came about, you can hear how huge the difference actually is. Not everything AJR makes is art just because we think of ourselves as artists; the world doesn't need to hear every unpolished track we've ever recorded. Undoubtedly, a lot of them are terrible. But when sharing successes, showing small but meaningful changes made along the way can be interesting or even illuminating for others, whether they are true fans or just smart observers who can understand and appreciate the difference—which might mean showing your best work in less-than-finished, less-than-perfect form.

Second, this level of transparency sometimes requires sharing things that some people might consider proprietary. We tend not to worry about that, even as Gen Z raises the bar on how much they expect artists, and everyone else, to share on the internet. On You-Tube, Ryan literally does a screenshare on his laptop and shows the waveforms in his Pro Tools window. He explains exactly how he engineers the instrumentation and effects that create AJR's sound, without any fear that he's giving too much away. Part of it is understanding that the art of production is just one element of our music. Plus, as Ryan said:

> I think that very often, by the time we put out an album, we're onto the next thing. What excites us constantly is that we're onto this new album and it's different from this last album.

In movement-building, the strengths of an organization are the resonance of the cause itself, the passion that leaders and supporters bring to it, and the tools used to amplify and steer all this energy that otherwise might run amok. The tools usually aren't proprietary. We all have access to the same social media platforms, the same poster board for protest signs, and so on. What's harder to replicate are the resonance and passion. And those are likely to spread when sharing the inside story of the movement and what it has accomplished. That's exactly what happened in the global youth climate movement, which only got traction in 2018 after a teenager in Sweden garnered international attention for skipping class and sitting outside Swedish parliament every school day to call for a serious reckoning with climate change. Greta Thunberg, who was fifteen at the time, introduced a new voice to the movement, with a mixture of rage and innocence and self-assuredness that captivated social media and the international press, giving her an incredible platform to share her story. She returned to school after the election but continued to strike with classmates on Fridays, and the #FridaysForFuture hashtag was born as a result. The campaign inspired students all around the world to start their own chapters of the movement, while

offering detailed guidance online for organizing action at the local
level.

TEACHING THE WAYS WITHOUT GETTING TOO TECHNICAL

Maybe because it was geared toward students from the beginning,
Fridays for Future has been notably adept at educating its audiences
without getting overly technical, avoiding a common pitfall for activists when it comes to giving people the inside story. It's simply
too easy for a general audience, or even one that's self-selected as
being interested in a particular cause, to bump up against an alienat-
ing amount of detail or jargon or complexity when learning about
important problems or potential solutions. I realize this sounds pa-
tronizing; I don't mean for it to be. As a professor, I genuinely believe in people's capacity to learn. But just briefly glance at the
United Nations' landmark reports on climate change (which come
out every six to seven years and run thousands of pages long), look
up any section of the federal tax code, consult the average medical
study on cancer research, or just visit a message board where engineers ask questions about using Pro Tools, and watch how quickly
things can get frighteningly technical, even for people with an interest in the topic.

Mark Rober, who parlayed an engineering career at NASA and
Apple into massive success as a YouTuber, keeps his reliably viral
popular-science videos far away from the technicality abyss, almost
instinctively. It's not just that the content is meant to be fun (you
might see him installing an obstacle course for the squirrels in his
yard, or whipping up oversized vats of "elephant toothpaste," or
creating glitter bombs that explode on neighborhood package
thieves). When he shares the mechanical or science-based details of
how he builds what he builds, he's just as engaging—and this as-

sessment is based not only on my personal opinion, but on something he told me when I asked him about this: The analytics show no drop-off in viewership between the explanatory segments of his videos and the high-impact (and often hilarious) results of his experiments. Here's what else Mark had to say about that:

> As far as engineers go, and science stuff, I am on the left side of the bell curve. I'm probably as far to the left in this genre as it gets. And that's because I do want to cast a wide net. A comment I actually get kind of often is "Oh, I wish you'd go more into the details of the thing." And my philosophy is, intentionally the stuff I do isn't that crazy. Like, the glitter bomb stuff—it's a custom-printed circuit board, sure. But it's, like, servo motors; it's not that hard programming-wise. There are lots of other channels that go deep into that stuff. But as soon as I go super deep for this techno nerd who wants all the details, I lose the mom or dad or kid who just isn't quite that detailed. And what I'm in the business of is getting people addicted to that aha moment, right? Someone may not remember the technical details of something I said, but a year later, they'll remember how they felt.

Movements also often thrive (at least temporarily) on moments that make people feel something—think giant marches, landmark Supreme Court rulings, or other important mileposts for catalyzing or measuring progress. These are the activist's version of the aha feeling in a Mark Rober science video, or the song explosion at the end of a Ryan-led production breakdown. Naturally, the big moments are the ones most likely to get documented by the media or by movement leaders and supporters themselves. But building resilient movements also involves an untold number of small moments—decisions that may have seemed inconsequential at the time, or the unexpected eureka moments that suddenly reframed everything. Skipping over the documenting of these small or surprising moments compromises the richness of the inside story about how the big moments transpired. That's why we record everything from the talkback mics when we're onstage for an AJR show—because you never know what's going to happen.

"THIS IS BIG"

Efrén Olivares learned this exact lesson when he was leading the racial and economic justice efforts of the Texas Civil Rights Project (TCRP). At the start of 2018, the nonprofit group was strongly focused on representing property owners at the U.S.-Mexico border whose lands interfered with the government's plans to build a border wall. But almost overnight, the TCRP found itself in the thick of an even more controversial component of Donald Trump's anti-immigration policy during his first White House term. Family separations at the border, which already had been tested in Arizona and El Paso, and had courted a class-action lawsuit in California, were in full swing by the spring of 2018 in McAllen, Texas, the border town where Efrén was based. It was nothing new for people who had come into the United States without authorization to end up in federal court in McAllen. But that May, a public defender in town told Efrén that she was noticing something unusual: Families that crossed the border were being separated, with the parents having no idea when, how, or even if they would be reunited with their children. The court in McAllen was so crowded at this point that the public, and even journalists, had trouble getting in. But as a lawyer, Efrén had access.

McAllen is home to just one of several courthouses along the Texas border with Mexico. It was not immediately clear that removal of children from the custody of their parents—many of whom had entered the United States seeking asylum and had done nothing illegal—had broadly become routine under the "zero tolerance" policy promulgated by the Trump administration that spring. But immigration advocates were starting to piece the story together. Efrén recalls going to his boss after visiting the courthouse one day in May 2018 and announcing: "This is big." Schools, community groups, and human rights institutions demanded the separation policy be reversed and the families reunited. It generated barely a ripple of reaction from the public. A few weeks later, Efrén stood outside the courthouse and, in a Facebook Live video, explained what he was learning inside the courthouse and requested help raising awareness.[4] This didn't do much to stir the public's consciousness either. As Efrén recalls:

> It was very frustrating not to see the level of outrage we thought was justified. What in the world are we doing as a society spending millions of dollars a year putting asylum seekers in cages? The usual suspects were supportive but it didn't spark outrage. That's why we tried to share as much of the stories that our clients would allow us to share in public. The turning point, finally, was when the audio came out.

The audio he's referring to was obtained by the nonprofit newsroom ProPublica, which published a leaked recording of children stuck inside a U.S. Customs and Border Protection detention facility, crying out over and over for their parents, who were being held separately.[5] Here's Efrén again:

I remember having conversations with my colleagues, saying, "One of these border patrol agents inside is going to end up leaking video of this." In the end, it was only the audio that came out. But I'm convinced that the reason the audio is so powerful is because it's audio, so you don't see the color of their skin. You only hear them cry, and all children cry the same, regardless of the color of their skin. . . . People were saying up until then that it's not the government's fault, that it's the parents' fault, that they shouldn't have brought them. But once they heard the audio, it became unacceptable in their minds.

The widespread press attention and public uproar Efrén had been waiting for had finally arrived. The leak was quickly amplified thanks mainly to things that nearly every movement has at its disposal these days: social media accounts and supporters with smartphones. Stung by criticism from around the world and from within his own party, Trump signed an executive order calling for the end of family separations at the border, just days after the recording of the children's cries went viral. But the TCRP's work on the issue was not over. Two days later, Efrén was back at the courthouse in McAllen, this time looking for signs that the government was being true to its word. He emerged and gave an impromptu press conference, shared via Facebook Live, during which he reported that he and his colleagues had interviewed more than 380 parents in the span of about five weeks, and that this was the first day he hadn't found any mothers or fathers saying they'd been newly separated from their kids.[6] At a time when the government was obfuscating, Efrén was offering some of the clearest pictures yet of the facts on the ground, and of his organization's involvement in the situation. He recalls:

I didn't have notes, I didn't have a plan. I just had the information that we had gotten from the court, and I shared it. . . . In retrospect, I hadn't been considering it as a particular type of strategy. But it was definitely a strategy, because of desperation. Nothing else was working.

Suddenly, the TCRP had a national platform. On July 5, 2018, *The New York Times* published an op-ed by Efrén, titled "A Day in the Life of a Lawyer at the Border." Contributions and grants to the TCRP poured in and totaled $9.4 million in 2018, far ahead of the $2.3 million received the year before.[7] The group would need the extra support to keep conducting and documenting its work; three years after Trump signed the executive order supposedly reversing the separation policy, more than two thousand children had yet to be reunited with their parents, and hundreds of additional families had been separated at the border. As for Efrén, he found yet another way to give people an inside look at his work on this issue: He wrote a memoir about his experience.

LIVE FROM MY DRESSING ROOM

Ryan, Mark, Greta, and Efrén were all highly intentional about what they shared and when, which allowed them to be transparent about their work without being dull and without ever crossing the line into oversharing. I kept their example in mind as I worked on this book, and on the TikTok account I created to support it.

Ah, TikTok. I resisted it for a long time, confining my presence there to videos posted by our AJR band account. But the first time I met with my publisher, he gently informed me that TikTok had become almost as important to the book industry as it was to the music industry. So I bit the bullet and started my own account.

My journey to figure out what and how much to share involved a lot of trial and error. I started by posting older clips of myself being interviewed on CNN, since I was too busy to make new content. It didn't work. I made straight-faced videos about climate change. It didn't work. I posted some music content. It didn't work. I shared books that I liked and disliked. It didn't work. Then I started to get more strategic about it. My thought process was roughly this:

- Climate, music, books: How can I deepen people's connections to these things?

- It might be smart to show how something is made, but only if the thing itself is interesting. What things are interesting to TikTok users? And how do those things overlap with what I do?

- How can I balance something technical with something that makes people feel something, so that they keep coming back for more content? Do I hide the climate stuff in something more fun?

- What can I show that would invite people to easily make their own versions? Instructional videos?

- And finally, what is on-brand enough that it won't feel like a departure from my real-life personality?

The answer was to do something I already do, and really like doing, and just film myself doing it. So I brought my electric hot pot to each stop on AJR's 2024 U.S. tour, and cooked something (usually, but not exclusively, Asian food) in my dressing room before or after every show. In each video, I highlighted the ingredients to make it easy for people to create their own versions. I snuck in facts about climate, talking about my compostable flatware or surprising farming practices. Sometimes I made dishes specific to whatever city we were in. I was sharing my love for food while offering basic technical advice for cooking it.

From the first video, I could tell the strategy was working. My measly little TikTok account with just a few hundred followers grew by the thousands over just a few weeks. I didn't abandon content about music, movements, climate, or books. Food became a gateway to videos about all of those other topics that are important to me. Suddenly my videos about collective action and my frustrations with recycling were getting just as many views as the ones where I made spicy peanut noodles in Grand Rapids, or sushi hand rolls in Minneapolis, or caramel apple "parfaits" (they didn't quite work out that way, but that was part of the fun) in Boise. The next thing I knew, fans were making their own TikToks trying out and reviewing my recipes, which allowed me to create duets in which I could react to their commentary. It was, I daresay, pretty fun. But it only worked when I approached it with intentionality, while remaining true to my interests and personality.

Spencer Barrett would say I was both *strategic* and *authentic,* the two qualities most likely to help anyone break through all the clutter on social media. And I trust what Spencer says about social media. In addition to his day job as a digital manager for an iconic American restaurant chain, he is a big Taylor Swift fan, and his supportive messages quoting her lyrics or celebrating her career milestones on his personal social media accounts first caught the attention of Taylor's marketing team more than a decade ago. (The next thing he knew, he was invited to meet the singer at her parents' house in Nashville, at a party celebrating the release of her *1989* album.) That's high praise, considering the care Taylor has famously put into her own social media presence, whether on MySpace in the early days, on Twitter during her *Red* era, on Tumblr when *1989* came out, or on TikTok, which she joined in 2021.

Platforms come and go, of course, and each offers unique features and access to different fan bases. What they all have in common, though, is what they ultimately demand of messengers who want to stand out. As Spencer said:

> It doesn't matter if you're Taylor Swift or if you're a restaurant brand or a movement. Are you showing up authentically on these platforms? How are you connecting with your target audience, your fan base, or your donors?
>
> It's so funny to say, but the thing that people forget sometimes about social media is it's supposed to be social. Yes, it's used for promoting your content, your work, your art, whatever it might be. But "come listen to my song," "come buy my food"—that's not interesting, that's not exciting. It's just going to get lost in all the noise. So how are you almost sneakily getting people involved in or thinking about your art, your content, or your brand? At the end of the day, it's about building relationships and connecting with other people.

I don't know if any of my videos on TikTok will ever have the virality of a Taylor Swift video. But would I even have gotten as much traction as I did if I weren't already in a band with an established fan base? We'll never know, as the algorithm is a black box. But if my status as a musician was that big a factor, then presumably my earlier videos would have done a lot better. On this platform, authenticity arguably matters more than celebrity. That should bode well for any movement that's ready to get transparent about the work they do and the causes they represent.

PRESS PLAY

COALESCE YOUR BASE WITH COOPERATION
AND FRIENDLY COMPETITION

With great confidence, I can say that a significant portion of the AJR fan base is evenly split between musical theater dorks and Dungeons & Dragons nerds. I've actually seen the data. (If you're a fan who doesn't feel like you fit into either one of these categories, trust me. Deep down, you know I'm right.)

I was raised mainly in the first camp, brought up on show tunes in our family's apartment not far from New York City's Theater District. But don't get me wrong: I also really love games.

161962343

There are two different animal species in AJR's video for "World's Smallest Violin," eight guests around the casino table in the video for "Bang!," and seven letters in the first name of the guy who calls out the lines "here we go" and "metronome" in "Bang!" (that would be radio veteran Charlie Pellett, whose voice we grew up with as New York City subway riders; his "Stand clear of the closing doors, please" is a public-transit classic). Each of those numbers (2, 8, and 7) were answers to just some of the AJR scavenger hunt questions we distributed across our social media channels. Those particular numbers corresponded to the letters "T," "H," and "E," which happened to spell the first word of a track that we released in 2022, "The DJ Is Crying for Help." If you had gone online, located all of the clues and their corresponding letters, found each bit of numerical information that the clues pointed to, put those numbers next to the appropriate letters, added up all the numbers in each word of the new song's title, and then tallied those six numbers together, you would get the nine-digit figure in the section header above, which was the password to a Zoom session where my brothers and I took questions and shared new music with the first one hundred fans to solve the puzzle and dial into the video call.

Like I said, I really love games.

In fact, the best twenty-four hours I ever had in college were spent in a role-playing simulation for a Columbia University course titled Oil, Rights, and Development. There were several dozen students in the class, and we were divided into roles representing an international industrial company, several factions of government, some nongovernmental organizations, members of the local community, and the media. Each role came with access to information or perspectives that only we had. Locked in a room together for the better part of two full days, we needed to figure out how much to share with the other parties, how to evaluate what was shared with us, and how to form alliances that would get to the best result possible for the fictitious country in which the storyline took place.

All these years later, having gotten a close look at real-life development issues through both my PhD research and my policy work, I still can't think of a better way to have learned about the various stakeholders commonly involved in these scenarios, or about tactics for forging a broad consensus. Though the project we debated in the class was just pretend, the stakes somehow felt high. As the hours flew by, I never once felt I was disengaged or lacking focus.

The simulation worked because it adhered to key principles of good game design, in that the exercise was participatory, the result was uncertain, and the players felt they could influence the outcome. But I wasn't aware of that at the time. What I knew was that I had just rapidly absorbed a bunch of really important lessons about some exceedingly complex topics, through an interactive exercise that was fun, creative, and memorable.

COLLABORATE WITH ME

The thrill I got from that class suggests I'm into the immersion of live-action role-play games, which probably explains the kinship I feel with the Dungeons & Dragons side of the AJR fan spectrum. And like most people, I also enjoy games that foster healthy competition. But the puzzles and challenges I'm drawn to most, as both a player of games and an occasional designer of them, are those that require collaboration.

Ahead of the release of the *OK Orchestra* album, we came up with the idea to scatter thirty-six individual jigsaw puzzle pieces across AJR's Twitter, Instagram, and Facebook accounts, and via our text and email lists, while a few were sent directly to select fans who were entrusted to somehow share their pieces with the rest of the fan community. Collecting every piece of the puzzle meant collaborating with fellow fans in different digital spaces; doing so allowed players to assemble the full puzzle, which revealed the album's track list. It wasn't as complex an operation as the scavenger hunt, but I would argue it was even more enjoyable because it had our fans working together, rather than competing directly. Then they, not us, shared the new track list with the world, which gave them a sense of ownership over it. For me and my brothers, watching our fans cooperate like this across platforms was a lot more fun than just posting the track list on our own.

In designing both that game and the scavenger hunt, we were guided mainly by instinct. But in working on this book a few years later, I finally had the chance to ask a games researcher—Katherine Isbister, a professor at the University of California, Santa Cruz, and the author of the book *How Games Move Us*—to explain why those AJR challenges seemed equally successful at engaging fans, even though one game emphasized competition and the other collaboration. This is what she told me:

> In both of those cases, you created suspense and interest. And even though the [track list] was collaborative, everyone individually wanted to see what it was, and wanted, probably, to be a meaningful part of revealing it. And also, there was the delightfulness of working on something together and having a shared experience.

Note that there is nothing in the professor's description of these kinds of games that is specific to the realm of music. Suspense, interest, shared experiences. Surely it doesn't take musicianship to create any of those things. But Katherine did observe that the music industry, similar to the video game industry, seems to understand how to "work with people's own impulses and half-formed goals and hopes and aspirations to move them into some interesting situation and make them feel like they've been a part of something." There are lots of ways music does this, of course, as you'll find throughout this book. But games, whether online or off (but especially online these days), have become an increasingly powerful component of fan engagement.

The fan motivators Katherine observed apparently work even at the scale of Taylor Swift. Ahead of the release of the *1989 (Taylor's Version)* album, fans searching Google for Taylor Swift one day in 2023 were presented with a game featuring eighty-nine different questions about the artist. Many started sharing their answers on spreadsheets and social media platforms. Within hours, players around the globe had collectively solved thirty-three million puzzles, which was the magic number to unlock the game's digital vault and reveal which of the singer's previously unreleased tracks would be included on the new album. (The game didn't break the internet, but it did briefly glitch, signaling the level of frenzy it generated.)[1]

WELCOME (BACK) TO DEMA

An even richer example of activating fans through play comes from Twenty One Pilots. The alt duo from Columbus, Ohio, built out an entire world that has been unlocked bit by bit, over several years and multiple albums, by followers solving puzzles and piecing together additional clues from track listings, song lyrics, and album cover art. Multiple Discord servers and YouTube channels run by fans are devoted to Twenty One Pilots' complicated lore, which features a shadowy figure called Blurryface (also the title of a 2015 Twenty One Pilots album) who represents lead singer Tyler Joseph's insecurities. Both Blurryface and Joseph's alter ego, Clancy, live in the dystopian city of Dema, which is ruled by nine bishops who will hunt down anyone who tries to escape. Would-be defectors may find themselves lucky enough to be aided by the Banditos, a group of helpers who dress in yellow because it's a color the bishops can't see. But those who are caught get sent back to Dema, where they are inculcated in the ways of Vialism, the brutal, made-up religion promoted by the bishops. It's all an allegory for Tyler's stark and very relatable struggles with the kinds of anxiety, depression, and intrusive thoughts that can prevent us from fulfilling our potential.[2]

Reinforced in both the storytelling and aesthetics of the band's music videos and concert stagings, the visual representations of this world are uncommonly rich, more akin to cinema than anything we might typically associate with a music artist, as Benjamin Stokes pointed out to me. Benjamin, a game designer and civic media scholar at American University, also noted that world-building itself isn't a requirement for creating a great game. (Sure enough, there's nothing about the design of Tetris or Wordle that was meant to transport players into an alternative universe.) To me, the genius of Twenty One Pilots' thoroughly detailed world-building is that it ties into well-designed games that encourage cooperation among fans.

According to Benjamin, the main things a game has to do to be great are:

- Invite playfulness

- Be participatory

- Offer an uncertain outcome

- Give players agency, or what feels like agency, to influence the outcome

- Let players know that the choices they make actually matter

So, let's look at the game Twenty One Pilots developed for the 2020 debut of the single "Level of Concern." Ahead of the release, the band's YouTube channel streamed live for twenty-four hours and revealed the address of a new website, along with a code that could be entered there. Each code unlocked a downloadable drive with pieces of a decoder and puzzles or clues to unlock the next drive. There were twenty drives in total. Many of the puzzles (a mix of crosswords, encryptions, map codes, you name it) were challenging for even the most dedicated Twenty One Pilots fans. Players worked together on various platforms, posting theories, tips, and hilarious observations about the difficulty and intricacy of the challenges. The final drive, once unlocked, pointed to yet another website. Here, fans were invited to upload footage to create a "never-ending video" for the new song; a fresh edit of the footage appeared each time the video looped.[3]

"Level of Concern" ended up being a moderate hit on the Billboard charts. For fans that participated in the twelve-plus hours of gaming to unlock the song, it was arguably much more than that.

WHY GAMES SHOULD MATTER TO MOVEMENTS

An estimated three billion people around the world play video games,[4] whether on mobile phones, PCs, or game consoles, constituting one of the largest global content audiences on Earth. And their interests aren't limited to slingshotting angry birds at green pigs, committing robberies in San Andreas, or guessing the track list to a new album based on a jumble of words provided by the artist (AJR did that last one in 2023 with the release of *The Maybe Man*). At the same time, video games, or at least some of them, have proven themselves quite adept at capturing emotional subtleties and cultural reflections, or even taking players on moral journeys, which more and more people are acknowledging. "It's kind of like how comics finally became graphic novels," said Katherine, the UC Santa Cruz professor. "There are so many more types of games that fit interesting niches now."

This all suggests a huge opportunity for movements, which have barely begun to experiment with using games to cultivate, educate, and activate their fan bases. Historically there have been some good reasons for the reluctance. Live-action role-playing simulations like the one I participated in at Columbia can be really fun and effective, and we're seeing them used for purposes ranging from war games to disaster preparedness. But they're hard to pull off and not very scalable. Video games might be a simpler option in that sense. But the toxic elements of traditional gamer culture have likely acted as a repellent here. Meanwhile, concrete evidence of the efficacy of games in a movement context is lacking. (A 2021 review of sixty-four research papers examining the impact of different gamification efforts related to climate found the games to have a positive effect on balance, but as the study noted, the engagements were short and the exact behavioral outcomes were unclear and difficult to measure and compare.)[5]

But there are equally good reasons for movement leaders to set these kinds of concerns aside, find games that align with their organization's goals, and dive in. For one thing, even simple games can incentivize a desired behavior. Taylor Swift knew this from her earliest days as an artist. "I think the first time that I started dropping sort of cryptic clues and things in my music was when I was fourteen or fifteen, putting together my first album, and I wanted to do something that incentivized fans to read the lyrics," she told Jimmy Fallon on NBC's *The Tonight Show* back in 2012, "because my lyrics are what I'm most proud about, of everything that I do, every aspect of my job. . . . I would have all lowercase-letter lyrics except for capital letter, capital letter, capital letter every once in a while, and if they circled the capital letters and wrote them down, it spelled out a secret code, a secret passage. It was really fun and it would tell them a story about the album or a hint about what the song was about."[6] Clearly her strategy worked.

Well-designed games and simulations could also be useful for movements when it comes to training people for specific roles, in the same way that there are simulators for pilots and firefighters. But even beyond that, games could be a great way for organizations to make sure they have people in the *right* roles. (And you'll remember from Chapter Two how important yet overlooked a task that is.) As Katherine at UC Santa Cruz told me:

> Something you might never do in normal life, you'll do within the "magic circle" of a game, because it's just a game. So, sure, you'll whack somebody with a foam hammer, when you would not do that in real life at all. Games allow people to try on different ways of being, if you design those moments right. It would be brilliant, for that role question, to ask somebody a few questions or let them play a little sim and see which character they enjoy the most.

Another opportunity for movements is to capitalize on the existence of game fans themselves—not necessarily to make games for them, but to address them as an audience and weave movement-related storylines into the content they consume, in the same way that there's currently a concerted effort in the film industry to work climate-change themes into movie scripts. There are other precedents for mixing campaigns with entertainment content. As a responsible citizen, you're probably familiar with the phrase "designated driver." But in 1988, most Americans weren't. That year, Harvard's Center for Health Communication went to all of the major television studios in Hollywood, and to the ABC, CBS, and NBC broadcast networks, with an idea to reduce traffic deaths and injuries related to drunk driving. With the blessing of the main screenwriters' union, TV writers over the next four years incorporated themes about drunk-driving prevention, especially the designated driver concept, into subplots and dialogue for more than 160 prime-time TV programs, including *Cheers, Dallas,* and *L.A. Law.* In that same time frame, alcohol-related traffic deaths dropped 25 percent, far outpacing the 5 percent drop in traffic fatalities unrelated to alcohol.[7] Where might a campaign look today to activate an audience at that scale? Gen Z isn't watching much prime-time TV. Zoomers are, however, tuning in to video-game streaming platforms like Twitch by the millions.

SUPER-INCUBATORS OF ENGAGEMENT

Another reason for movements to be thinking a lot more about play, and the one I'm most excited about as a big fan of collaborative games, is that movements thrive when they can build connections among supporters, and games are remarkably useful for that. Just ask Phil Keslin, a co-founder of the game studio that created Pokémon GO. That's what I did, and if you have read Chapter One, then you will know how excited I was for this interview.

> One of the things that we discovered with Pokémon GO is that if you can connect a player with another player in the game—I mean actually connect them in real life— then the likelihood that they will continue playing the game in the long run goes up dramatically. It's really profound. And my personal belief is it's because of the interaction between those two people.

Actually, with a game like Pokémon GO, the real-world interactions often involve way more than two people. At Pokémon GO Fests hosted by Niantic Labs (Phil is the company's chief technology officer), tens of thousands of Pokémon GO players will descend on a city for three days of play. But it doesn't require a big event like that to see how a game can have a big impact, especially at the community or family level. Prior to the app's debut in 2016, Phil "never saw families going for walks" in his Northern California neighborhood, he told me.

> It wasn't until Pokémon GO came out that we saw Mom, Dad, and the kids walking around the neighborhood for an hour every night after dinner. Instead of watching television or going to two different locations—the kids watch their shows and mom and dad watch their shows— families were connecting in a way that they hadn't in a while, and that to me was really powerful.

Phil's team likes working in what he called the "liminal space between the real world and the game world," and creating challenges that require players to access both realms.

> What is it about that, that gets people so excited? The only thing I can think of is the interaction with other people who enjoy it just as much. Why did I play Dungeons & Dragons? It's because I liked the fantasy part of it, and I'm surrounded by people who also enjoy it.

See? D&D or musical theater. It's always one or the other.

Anyway, a few years before Phil's team came out with Pokémon GO, the group, which was a part of Google at the time, developed a game called Ingress, an augmented reality adventure with a smaller but cultishly devoted following known to go to unusual lengths in the name of play. Once, a group of players collected enough money to charter a bush plane in Alaska, so they could physically fly a gamer to a remote town where she could digitally break up an imaginary blockade stretching along the U.S. West Coast, as part of a special game within the game. "Oh my *god*," Phil said, invoking the drama of the situation as he described what happened next.

> If you listen to the radio conversation about it, it sounds like a military operation. But it's just a group of people that are playing a game. We had this little party after it was over, and I just remember people saying it was the most fun they ever had. And the thing that made it fun was the engagement with other people.

Sometimes the engagement was literal:

> We get these postcards from people who met each other in the game and then they got married and then they had a kid, and then they named their kid after one of the characters [in Ingress]; we've had quite a bit of that. Or sometimes somebody's down on their luck, but after playing games with these people for several years, now they have a couch to sleep on until they can get back on their feet.

Though it probably has the tools to do so, Niantic isn't using its games in an attempt to spread any particular values or messages beyond the company's stated mission of getting people to go outside, explore their communities, get some exercise, and find connection. But already it has proven that well-designed games have the power to do that much, which a) is no small thing, and b) might be inspiring to organizations involved in any number of causes, but especially civic organizations that might share one or more of the goals espoused by Niantic.

FRICTION AND FEEDBACK

Benjamin, the games scholar at American University we heard from earlier, is the director of the school's Playful City Lab, which has worked with Niantic, along with a variety of foundations and civic institutions, to investigate how play can fortify communities, advance equity, and create or strengthen a sense of local identity. He also co-founded Games for Change, a nonprofit that promotes and supports the use of games for social innovation. According to Benjamin, there is plenty of untapped potential for movements of all kinds to build and activate support through play. But he called out two potential problem areas for incorporating games in the movement space.

First, good games require something that is anathema to most movements: friction. Most movements spend a lot of time and energy on reducing friction. They want to quickly sign up as many supporters as they can; they want to give people tools that make it easy to donate money, participate in campaigns, or send messages to political representatives. Good games, however, purposefully incorporate friction, playing around with the pacing or the level of challenge to keep players on their toes.

Second, Benjamin said, good games "tell stories partly by giving people choices, or at least a feeling of choice," and that's important. But so is "amplifying that sense of agency by giving people feedback when they make a choice." And here, many movements don't have a great track record, Benjamin said.

> We often forget that people really want to get confirmation of "Oh, yes, you took this action six months ago, and the campaign is over, but we want to affirm that choice that you made to participate." Game design tells

us that that's a really important feedback loop to close. And we're often ending the feedback loops way too early [in movements] because we built them around campaigns, and not necessarily around sustaining engagement. And we know that the campaigns on climate are going to keep beginning and ending, and beginning and ending, because it's not going to be done in two years. So I think some of the principles of games can be helpful for thinking across campaigns.

Friction. Feedback. Okay, got it. Let's now return for a moment to that Twenty One Pilots game, just to appreciate how seamlessly it incorporated both of these things. As fans can attest, the friction was real, and it varied in its intensity. Some of the puzzles, such as the word search featuring names of the band's songs, were much easier to complete than others, like the string of numbers that needed to be plugged into a decimal-to-ASCII converter to produce a code to unlock the next drive (and clues in other drives got way more complicated from there).[8]

As for feedback to affirm the players' actions? Well, there was the immediate payoff of being invited to upload footage for the never-ending video for "Level of Concern," and being able to see other fans' (and the band's) footage mixed in with their own. Plus, the whole time in the background, there was the excitement of knowing that the lore underpinning the 2020 game had very likely been shaped at least in part by the fan base. As Tyler Joseph had acknowledged in an interview two years earlier with Zane Lowe for Apple Music, when Twenty One Pilots released its *Trench* album: "I don't think they [the fans] know how much they've written the narrative, and how much of a back-and-forth we've been having without them really even being fully aware. . . . They helped create this world as well." For instance, Tyler said, the character of Blurryface, which originally represented a mirror reflecting back our faults, had morphed into a commentary about jurisdiction, and avoiding the grip of our insecurities by staying away, physically or mentally, from the places where Blurryface has control. This change, he suggested, was the result of carefully watching the internet to see how fans that "really, really get it" were viewing the character, and realizing he "agree[d] with them on how he's perceived."[9]

As for how he sees or hears the different interpretations of this world he has created, Tyler told Lowe, "It is the internet, man. I'm around."[10] For fans that have contributed to the discourse on Blurryface, could there be more exciting feedback, or greater affirmation that their participation mattered, than that?

AN IMPORTANT CAVEAT

While I'd like to see movements borrow a page from musicians and use games to engage their fan bases, I feel compelled to issue a caveat: Even well-resourced experts sometimes design games that flop.

Niantic figured it had a surefire hit when it launched *Harry Potter: Wizards Unite* in 2019, but it shut the whole game down less than three years later. Why didn't this one catch on with players? "Well, I don't know that we actually know why," Phil Keslin told me. (His speculation is that broad, deep knowledge of the Harry Potter story left little room for the playfulness or uncertain outcomes that help keep games engaging.)

Having overseen massive hits as well as a few failures, Phil said his best advice is: "Iterate quickly." He often advises developers to eschew lengthy prototyping early on and instead use low-tech mechanisms like pen and paper or pushpins and Post-it Notes to

quickly gauge whether a game concept makes sense and can grab
people.

> One thing that we have discovered is [how to] build
> something and try it. Give it to a bunch of people, a di-
> verse group of people, and let them try it—people who
> aren't gamers, who are gamers—and just see what hap-
> pens. If there's some little spark there, then you can refine
> it more. But if it just fails—if [it's a mobile game and]
> everybody puts the phone down—then you know you've
> hit a wall and you should just start over.

I asked Phil, hypothetically, if I wanted to teach people about the
five main sources of carbon emissions that are worsening climate
change (for the record, that's agriculture, production, construction,
transportation, and energy), could I perhaps get them excited to
learn through an app-based game that would require them to run
around the real world helping to install transmission lines and solar
panels or regenerative agriculture practices?

"I don't know," he said, his thoughtful expression suddenly
turning into a wry smile. "Try it."

OKAY, LET'S TRY IT

Literally. Let's try something. (Not my hypothetical above; that's
too ambitious for right now, but maybe we can play it someday
soon.) In this chapter, we learned about a handful of different strategies for game-building, and while we don't have the space and time
to build new worlds, we may be able to employ a few of these techniques to teach a historic fact about climate action, in a hopefully
memorable way.

In the United States, one of the biggest misconceptions about climate change is that it is an issue that divides the country along partisan lines. This is not true. Politically, the population is pretty evenly divided. But close to 75 percent of the American public believes climate change is real, and most of these people agree we're not doing enough about it.[11] Because we're not doing enough about it, we don't realize that there are so many other people around us who also care about it. We are often afraid to talk about it, because we're worried our friends, families, and neighbors will disagree with us, and that this will lead to fraught relationships.

Research tells us that one of the most effective things that any one person can do in support of climate action is talk more about climate change, with a sense of hope and optimism for the future.[12] The aim is not to convince the nonbelievers, but to make climate change the subject of enough dinner table conversations that it becomes a more significant part of the national conversation. But what can you talk about that is light enough for the whole family, important enough that it's not a waste of time, and surprising enough that people may remember it? Let's find out.

- What was the model number of the Ford truck pulling the parade float that Maxwell Frost stood on in 2013? Hint: Check the foreword to this book.

- Subtract the number of seasons that *Bill Nye the Science Guy* ran on television. Hint: See Chapter Two.

- Next, subtract the length of Tracy Chapman's song "Fast Car" (in minutes only; don't worry about the seconds). Hint: We discussed it in Chapter Three.

- Add that number to the number of pilots in the band name referenced in this chapter.

- Add that to the sum of all the single digits in the password used to access AJR's 2022 track release.

- Then, subtract the number of letters in the full legal name (first, middle, last) of the artist who created eighty-nine questions for a game on Google.

- Finally, add the number of the chapter in this book where I mention the Billion Oyster Project, multiplied by 16.

This answer, if you calculated correctly, is the number of countries that agreed to the Paris Agreement, the pivotal international treaty that Christiana Figueres (from Chapter Two) negotiated in 2015. Maybe you didn't know that this many countries even existed! But, if you did this correctly, you would know that pretty much the entire world agrees that climate change is a problem. Plus now you have a new fact to share that you are far more likely to remember simply because you figured it out for yourself (but if you don't want to do all that work, it is also the same as the first three digits of the first year of Billboard Hot 100 songs examined in the song compressibility study we looked at in Chapter Three).

This tiny version of a game is just the beginning of what movements can do to engage people in creative ways. Engagement, suspense, shared experiences, a sense of ownership—these are all important drivers of gameplay. Fostering collaboration or competition around them can help movements move people, first toward participation, and ultimately to action.

ALIVE NATION

MAXIMIZE THE ENDURING POWER OF GATHERING IN PERSON

Two of the most fun shows I've ever played took place in a stadium parking lot in Philadelphia in 2020, during the first summer of the Covid-19 pandemic. Each night, nine hundred cars full of fans were instructed to park in staggered formation, their radios tuned to a station that would broadcast our live performance from a mobile stage at one end of the lot. There were no speakers on the stage or anywhere outdoors, which meant we could barely hear ourselves play. If the audience was singing along or applauding in their socially distanced vehicles, we couldn't hear that either. It was as though we were playing into a void. I realize this all sounds more strange than fun. And for the first three songs on night one, that was absolutely the case. And then, the honking started.

I don't know about you, but I'd never associated the sound of a blaring car horn with anything positive. Honking is for when you're angry, impatient, or afraid. It's a purposefully jarring, annoying sound that says "Speed up!" or "Look out!" or "Screw you!" But at these concerts, the honking—first with one car, then dozens, then hundreds—became a way for the audience, so noticeably separated from us and from one another, to collectively communicate their appreciation and excitement after each song. Once I realized what was happening, it was a beautiful sound to my ears.

Okay, I promise this is not a chapter about rediscovering the joy of live performance in the middle of a global pandemic. Obviously, after months of being stuck at home, it was going to feel great to get back onstage and entertain a crowd, even if the configuration was vastly different from a normal concert. Surely our fans were elated to come together for a fun event during a dark time, and certainly I've never been part of a show that has felt more necessary. But while the concept for the "A Night in Your Car with AJR" shows might never have come about without a pandemic, with some distance I've realized the dreadful circumstances were purely incidental to the two most important lessons I took from the experience:

1. In-person events still matter, even in our increasingly digital age.
2. We can make more impact when we raise the bar on what a live event can be and what it offers the audience.

In this chapter, we'll look at what the music industry understands so well about live events, and what the world of social activism can learn from it. We'll look at the best uses for live events and the reasons they sometimes fall flat, and we'll examine some inspiring ways to reimagine the experience of an in-person gathering, whether you're bringing people together to raise money, spread awareness, mobilize support, celebrate wins, or establish new behaviors that will further the movement's mission.

WHY MOVEMENTS NEED LIVE EVENTS

In theory, the digital revolution should have wiped out the need for in-person gatherings. Why go to a concert when you can find footage of your favorite artists on the internet? Why march in the streets when you can sign an online petition? Why host an annual fundraising dinner when you can solicit donations all year via email? As both an artist and a nonprofit founder who is a) not a Luddite, and b) has to think about budgets, I grapple with these kinds of questions a lot. And in each case, I think the answer comes down to two words: "collective effervescence."

Émile Durkheim, a French sociologist, coined the term more than a century ago, although the concept has existed pretty much since the dawn of human existence. Collective effervescence is the feeling of everyone in an audience being on the same wavelength. It's the electricity in the air. It materializes whenever a group is bound together by excitement, joy, anticipation, indignation, anger, resolve, or really any emotion (positive or negative) that grows more visceral and potent when shared between people. Durkheim's work on the concept focused mainly on the atmosphere of religious rituals. But concerts, sporting events, political rallies—really any scenario that pulls together a crowd and unites them emotionally— can create this kind of energy. While there's no guarantee of a happy outcome (the insurrection at the U.S. Capitol on January 6, 2021, comes to mind), collective effervescence is what produces the feeling of being swept up in the moment, when that moment includes other people.

After playing hundreds of dates in cities around the world and encountering a lot of concert-induced effervescence along the way, I still find it hard to articulate what this palpable energy feels like from the stage. But as Supreme Court justice Potter Stewart famously said about pornography, I know it when I see it. I also know there is way more than one formula for creating it. I've witnessed collective effervescence at concerts in small clubs and in giant arenas, at shows packed with fans who scream out every lyric, and in places where custom dictates very different behavior. In Japan, for example, concert audiences tend to listen in attentive silence and applaud politely. Nothing raucous or thunderous is happening. And yet the effervescence is there.

Ben Folds, the veteran alt-rock musician who toured in the 1990s with the band Ben Folds Five and has performed live for decades in support of solo projects, told me he's not only aware of the crowd energy—sometimes he even finds himself in conversation with it. Usually that happens on the occasions when he goes against everything he learned from his band teachers at school and subconsciously speeds up the tempo of a song while he's performing it live. This is not an uncommon occurrence for musicians who play without recorded tracks or a click (metronome) in the background keeping the pace. It's just a by-product of the excitement of live performance. Sometimes the audience is fine with the tempo changes, and sometimes it isn't. Ben listens to what the room is telling him and abides by the wishes of the collective.

> I care what the feeling is, what the collective feeling is. . . . So if I'm rushing, and I feel like "actually, it's a room of seventh-grade band teachers, and they don't agree with that," then I can feel the power of the collective pulling me back—because I do want to communicate, or maybe I want to please, but there is a communication that's two-way. I am a man of science, let it be known. I don't get real, you know, abstract about those things. But you feel it for whatever reason.

Though the energy of a good crowd is intangible, it isn't totally immeasurable. In addition to decades of social science research showing self-reported increases in the intensity of emotions people experience while part of a crowd, studies of changes in brain activity have demonstrated that when people take part in experiences together, the neural firings in their brains actually start to synchronize.[1] Musicians have always understood this. Well, maybe not the brain-waves part. But they wouldn't be surprised to learn the facts about that. When a drummer cracks a pair of drumsticks together in the air to set a beat for the audience to clap along to, they are summoning collective effervescence. When a singer thrusts the microphone toward the crowd to signal that everyone should sing together, they are tapping into the collective effervescence and heightening it. Sports is another area of cultural life that regularly generates mass quantities of collective effervescence, between both the competition on the field and all of the pageantry baked into the live events—from the marching bands at a college football game, to the rallying cries of fans in the stands at a soccer stadium, to baseball's seventh-inning stretch.

Durkheim proposed that when people come together, not only do their emotions heighten, but their individual consciousness takes a back seat to group consciousness, and the social cohesion enhances their sense of belonging.[2] The atmosphere of togetherness also creates what social scientists call "collective efficacy," the feeling that it's more possible to get something done when you do it as part of a group. Forget putting on a concert. These are ripe conditions for persuading people to do things for the betterment of society! And that's why movements should be embracing and improving live events—because while the technology for digital events keeps getting better and better, there's nothing like the intensity of a physical experience to compel people to action.

CLEARLY DEFINE THE MISSION

There are several historic examples of movements and musicians coming together to put on live events in the hopes of generating collective effervescence that will lead to collective action. One of the first done at any scale in response to a humanitarian crisis was the 1971 Concert for Bangladesh at Madison Square Garden, organized by musicians George Harrison and Ravi Shankar, in partnership with UNICEF. An even more ambitious undertaking arrived the following decade with Live Aid, the transatlantic 1985 concert to raise money for Ethiopian famine relief. More than seventy-five of the biggest pop and rock acts of the era simultaneously descended on Wembley Stadium in London and JFK Stadium in Philadelphia for a sixteen-hour show attended live by a combined 162,000 people and watched on television by another 1.9 billion worldwide. The telethon-style event raised an estimated $140 million, roughly $400 million in today's dollars after adjusting for inflation.[3]

The success of Live Aid triggered a wave of other notable concert events. Later that year, John Mellencamp, Willie Nelson, and Neil Young organized the first Farm Aid concert, benefiting family farmers. Back at Wembley in London, music fans gathered for a succession of similarly styled events in the late 1980s and 1990s and through the mid-aughts, including two concert tributes to Nelson Mandela and the 1992 Freddie Mercury Tribute Concert for AIDS.

Wendy Laister, who ran global marketing and publicity campaigns for several of these concerts before becoming a full-time manager to bands including Duran Duran, said the most successful of these big, live events had a simple message and a clear, discrete mission centered around either fundraising, awareness-raising, or celebrating. With the failed attempts, she said, and there were several of those, usually it wasn't clear what the message was or what the audience was being asked to do. Without those fundamentals, it's impossible to create impact, even if the event comes with a stellar lineup of artists, and especially when those artists are, say, flying in on private jets for a concert about climate action. But let's stick here to the successful stuff. In the case of the first Mandela concert, where Sting, Peter Gabriel, Stevie Wonder, Tracy Chapman, and dozens of other top-tier performers were jammed into an eleven-hour show, the mission was to draw attention to the then-ongoing imprisonment of South Africa's leading anti-apartheid activist, on the occasion of his seventieth birthday.[4] The event was widely credited with achieving the objective. As Wendy recounted it:

> It gave a wide stage to something that was an issue, but one that was not necessarily on everybody's agenda. It wasn't a fundraiser. It was very much about awareness, and . . . it absolutely helped put pressure on governments around the world [to press for Mandela's release] because there was just so much public debate about it.

In 1990, an all-star bill assembled once again at Wembley. The clearly defined mission this time? Celebration. After twenty-seven years in prison, Mandela had been freed. He attended the show in person and spent forty-five minutes onstage, during which he received an eight-minute standing ovation, called for continued pressure on South African apartheid, and harkened back to the success and purpose of the event held in his honor two years prior.[5] "I would like to take advantage of this occasion to extend our special thanks to the artists of the world who have, for many years, lent their talents to the common effort to end the apartheid system," Mandela said. "We thank you especially for what you did to mark our seventieth birthday. What you did then made it possible for us all to do what we are doing here today."[6]

MINUS THE MUSIC

Of course, movements can't always rely on musicians to build collective effervescence for them. Luckily, they don't need to. With in-person events calibrated correctly for their purpose and their audience, movements have the capacity to create this energy all on their own.

For a great example of this, look no further than Pride. All over the world, chapters of this spirited LGBTQIA+ movement orchestrate events that often feel like a wild party while still somehow communicating the serious equal-rights issues at stake. Part of the magic of Pride is its focus on celebration, which, as Wendy said, is one of the key missions that pair particularly well with live events.

Celebration feels good, and we probably don't do enough of it in the movement world. Besides providing a well-deserved pat on the back to the movement participants or allies responsible for a win, a proper celebration can be an investment in the movement's growth. Wins are a terrific marketing tool, if you actually market them. People want to join movements when they see that an achievement is possible, that it's not always a slog against external forces likely to prevent you from ever getting anywhere. While researchers have found that celebrations and demonstrations are both good at creating conditions conducive to collective action, collective *efficacy*—the group's belief in its ability to achieve its goals—was more strongly associated with celebrations than demonstrations.

The purpose of Pride isn't limited to celebration, though, which is another reason why the events are so consistently successful—

they move with the times. According to NYC Pride co-chair Sue Doster, the crowd at New York City's Pride March was even bigger in 2017, the year Donald Trump was inaugurated for his first term as U.S. president, than in 2015, the year the U.S. Supreme Court legalized gay marriage nationwide. Here's Sue:

> The first Pride after [Trump] was elected was one of the largest Prides we had in history. The community really did come together. Pride was originally born of protest. There's still that vein that runs through it today. And people felt like it was important to show up and turn out.
>
> Pride is very organic. It swells and wanes. We'll see more involvement in election years when these issues are definitely [at the forefront]. In some ways, it's a living organism, and it expands and contracts and flows a little.

That flexibility even extends to how Pride is commemorated across geographies and cultures. In New York, the centerpiece is the parade, of course. It's the largest Pride event in North America. (São Paulo lays claim to the world's largest.) But in some cities with Pride celebrations, there's no parade at all. As Sue said:

> Pride meets people where they are, and it reflects the local attitudes and vibes. So, New York City: big city, we're a big march. But in Montgomery, Alabama, Pride is more about having a big picnic and bringing everybody together. Jersey Pride, it's mostly a small parade leading into a festival with a stage. Even in hostile climates for Pride, Pride finds a way. In India, instead of having marches in the streets, they have film festivals, where their people can feel comfortable in a dark theater, be-

cause the threat is real if they're out marching in the street. So Pride finds a way, just like music finds a way. Fans find a way.

Fans do find a way. That's precisely what I realized at those drive-in concerts, when the car horns started honking. No one instructed anyone to do that; it was just the fans adapting, and then contributing, to a new collective experience, designed for the era in which it took place.

LET'S REIMAGINE LIVE EVENTS

The way my brothers and I have always seen it, a perfect show is one that keeps you so engrossed that you can't look away for even a minute. We want you to feel amazement, surprise, wonder— basically any sensation that helps you overpower the urge to mindlessly scroll your phone. Our 2024 arena tour had us popping out of "toasters" under the floor that launched us onto the stage, and running up to the nosebleed seats every night to perform "World's Smallest Violin" from the stands. Jack was suspended from the ceiling for multiple numbers, as special effects made it look like he was skydiving his way through "Karma" and escaping danger like an action hero in "Yes I'm a Mess." We had comedy segments and shadow puppets and ad-libbed banter with the audience. The pacing was so frenetic that there was always a chance it could be a bit too much. But the concert reviews and, more important to us, the fan feedback we observed at the shows and online afterward, indicated otherwise.

Your organization might not be holding arena-sized events, but there are still many practices I've come across in the contexts of music and movements that are all too rare and well worth replicating if we want live events that are relevant and resonant—and I promise they don't require big venues, expensive staging, a lick of music, or any special effects.

MAKE IT COMFORTABLE

If you've been to an AJR show, then you know my brother Jack can dance rather . . . wildly. It's a wonder he can sing that way, running up and down and across the stage, jumping, spinning, limbs constantly flailing. I'll let him explain why he does it:

> I get pretty physical, yeah. It's all really purposeful. I mean, I've been going to concerts a really long time and they're really an awkward place to be. It is not a comfortable environment in the slightest for anyone. I used to notice that and I assumed, "Wait a sec—if I look like the most ridiculous person here, then maybe the audience will start to come out of their shells a little bit. At least they won't be as dumb-looking as me, so they can maybe start to move and have a good time and not care how they look."
>
> Bruce Springsteen and Billy Joel, all these veterans, they're just so good at relaxing the crowd and letting them know they're in good hands. And then you really feel that you could sing alongside a stranger, and those are the best shows.

Contrast that environment with another common setting for fundraisers: the black-tie dinner. These upscale events are typically planned and executed with the precision of a well-staged concert.

But you can tell they're not designed to set people at ease. Consider this all-too-common scenario:

1. You walk into a giant, noisy room for the cocktail hour, all dressed up and unsure of who to talk to or what to say, or how to gracefully eat hors d'oeuvres while balancing a drink in your hand.
2. You're finally seated at a table. You meet a small group of interesting people and wish you'd met them first instead of spending all that time in the cocktail hour milling around aimlessly. But just as the conversation gets going, you're shushed because the formal program has started.
3. After many speeches and an uninteresting meal, you're turned back out onto the street, possibly in your least comfortable shoes (unless, like me, you wear sneakers with basically everything, which I highly recommend but also recognize as a mostly male privilege).

Or maybe you're figuratively and literally well-suited for these kinds of events, in which case, forget what I just said. You'll be fine. But check on your fellow attendees, especially the introverts. They might be having an awkward time.

MAKE IT ACCESSIBLE

The average ticket price across the world's top 100 concert tours first surpassed the $100 mark in 2022, according to *Pollstar*, a trade publication for the live music industry.[7] Then came a wave of sellout stadium shows by acts like Taylor Swift, Bruce Springsteen, and Beyoncé. By the third quarter of 2023, the average ticket price had shot up another 20 percent to $122.84,[8] which of course is just a fraction of what it might cost to get floor seats at a major venue in any big city. My brothers and I hate the idea of this kind of sticker shock preventing people from coming to AJR shows. It just doesn't sit well with us from a moral perspective, let alone given how important touring has been to people's discovery of our music and to the growth of our fan base. So at every headline show we do, we price at least a handful of tickets at $35 plus venue fees. They're admittedly not the most desirable seats. But they're well within range of the collective effervescence in the air, which doesn't just suddenly end at the loge level with the people in luxury suites. Plus, we just might show up in your section to play a song or two, as we've been known to do.

Of course, cost isn't the only way to think about making things accessible to people. More broadly, our goal is maintaining low barriers to entry. A parallel to this in the movement world is promoting low-effort actions that still have demonstrable impact, like voting. If you're eligible to participate in elections, then this is one of the easiest things you can do to help realize change in the world. Registered voters can help elect candidates with sound climate policies, for example, which would have a far greater impact on our climate future than recycling at home. Once you register, there's some periodic follow-up required; you do actually have to exercise your vote for it to count. But you could spend a lot more time and effort every year separating your trash, with way fewer benefits to society. Protesting in the streets is one way for movements to get people participating in live events. But a voter drive involves a much lower barrier to entry. With millions of eligible Americans still not registered to vote, and Democratic voter turnout having fallen in 2024, there's a huge opportunity for movements to set up tables at live events and help get people registered and to the polls by showing them exactly what to do, and how easy it is to do it.

MAKE IT FUN

In Portland, Oregon, a phys ed teacher named Sam Balto organized a series of amazing in-person events that simultaneously get kids and parents exercising, reduce carbon emissions, solve a transportation problem for families without school bus access, and bring neighbors together. On specific days, the "bike bus" has students cycling to their elementary school instead of taking the school bus. Kids are picked up at stops along a specified route emphasizing greenways with traffic diverters and twenty-miles-per-hour speed limits. Sometimes parents will join in and cycle off to work after the kids lock up their bikes at school. Along the route, neighbors pop out of their houses to wave at everyone and wish them well. On a ride I was invited to join when AJR swung through Portland on tour in 2024, more than 150 people took part.[9] The bike bus isn't just a (literal) rolling advertisement raising awareness about the change Balto wants to see in the world; it *is* the change. And it's low-cost, easily replicable, and really fun to do.

MAKE IT LAST

A cynical theory of the music industry's obsession with merch would simply note that for touring bands, concert merch is a rather important moneymaker. Or, we could go back to Durkheim, who wrote in 1912: "Without symbols, social sentiments could have only a precarious existence. . . . But if the movements by which these sentiments are expressed are connected with something that endures, the sentiments themselves become more durable."[10]

So Durkheim was a merch guy! What our French sociologist friend was referring to are the emblems of collective experience, imbued with special meaning because they were part of the ritual. In other words, a T-shirt is just a T-shirt. But when it's a T-shirt from a concert you saw with your best friend, emblazoned with the names or faces or tour dates of your favorite act—or perhaps one that was ordered via app and delivered to your car during that drive-in show you surreally saw in the middle of a pandemic—it's suddenly a lot more meaningful than a random T-shirt you could buy at Target. (It's also probably going to cost you a lot more, and for that I'm sorry. But your patronage is appreciated.)

The takeaway here for movements is not that they need to have merch, though many organizations do, and some of them are quite clever about it. The takeaway is that it's important to leave people with something that keeps them connected to the cause long after your initial interaction with them has ended. Merch is one way to do this. (As Durkheim noted, when an emblem of collective effervescence stirs up the participants' memories of the experience, "it is as though the cause which excited them in the first place continued to act.")[11] But there are other ways to encourage ongoing participation in a movement. You could, for example, solicit sign-ups for movement-related actions taking place further out on the calendar. Or you could provide people with talking points or facts and figures that they could then use to help bring others into the fold. You could even borrow a strategy from Planet Reimagined and give people a QR code linking them to all of those things—local volunteer opportunities, information meant to be passed along to friends and family, plus voter registration instructions and links to important online petitions. Put the QR code on a postcard, and you've given people an emblem commemorating their participation at the initial event while furthering the odds that they stay actively connected to the cause.

BEFORE YOU GO

I'm going to take a bit of my own advice here and leave you with something: a checklist for your next in-person event. There's no need for all of these boxes to be checked. Even one or two check marks can suggest the gathering is being designed in a thoughtful way.

- ✓ Is the mission clear? (celebration, protest, awareness-building, etc.)

- ✓ Is there an ask being made of the participants?

- ✓ If so, is it clear? Simple? Specific?

- ✓ Is it easy for people to participate?

- ✓ Is it a comfortable environment for participants?

- ✓ Is it fun?

- ✓ Is there a way for people to take the mission home with them?

  Now go forth and live (with a long "i").

GRACELAND

RECOGNIZING THE FULL, COMPLICATED
BREADTH OF YOUR AUDIENCE

One of the advantages of having AJR grow as slowly and me-
thodically as it did was that we never had to confront the
problem of the sophomore slump. That's what it's called when a
musician explodes onto the scene with a debut album, only to see
their follow-up flop. There are lots of reasons why some artists are
cursed this way, but a big one is that if you rush out a second album
to capitalize on the success of the first, you probably don't have the
time you need to engage in active listening, to find out specifically
what it is that fans actually like about you or your music.

When you're building a fan base for the long term, whether for
a band or a movement, you can't go with your gut that you know
who your followers are, what they want, or why they like you.
These are things you need to learn and relearn, with every new
album, tour, event, or campaign you create. At meet-and-greets before concerts, we love hearing directly from fans about what's reso-
nating with them. And of course sites like YouTube offer a wealth of

information about how people feel, for better or worse, about every bit of work we share with the world.

In studying those reactions, we've also learned a lot about the fans themselves—their demographics, their worldviews, their influences. They really run the gamut, so I'm aware our audience is not a monolith. But I was never expecting to find out that our fan base stretched wide enough to include right-wing political commentator Glenn Beck.

FACE-TO-FACE WITH A FAN

"So, how surprised were you when you saw that tweet?"

My answer: *Very.*

The tweet in question was one that Glenn had posted shortly past midnight after an AJR concert in Dallas in 2022. And the person asking me about it, two years later in a meeting at his office, was Glenn himself.

If you're not familiar with Glenn, think of him as an early-2000s precursor to political agitator Tucker Carlson. Both rose to fame as provocative television hosts on CNN before landing nightly shows at Fox News, where they peddled angry Republican rhetoric and unfounded conspiracy theories to disturbingly large audiences. And both got fired at the peak of their popularity, having taken things too far even for their bosses at Fox. Glenn's rise and fall predated the cancellation of *Tucker Carlson Tonight* by more than a decade, but he remains a conservative firebrand.

So, yes. I was extremely surprised by Glenn's tweet calling us "GREAT song writers, performers and lyricists" and praising our performance as "fun and positive." I was also genuinely touched by it—not because of the compliments he paid to the band but because of what he wrote next: "I began to understand my son through their music years ago. SEE THEM if near you. THX AJR."[1]

Clearly I had more to learn about our fans.

KNOW YOUR AUDIENCE

AJR's audience isn't especially concentrated in any single age bracket, gender, or geographical region. But we're known for attracting a *type*. Kind and supportive, maybe a bit alternative, probably familiar with the experience my brothers and I all had at one time or another of feeling like an outsider and, maybe because of that, open to learning about other people's points of view—that's an apt way to describe so many of the fans I've met over the years. The description could certainly apply to Glenn's son, Raphe, who discovered AJR's music in his early teens. Over the course of my four-hour visit with Glenn, Raphe stopped in several times while spending the day working at his dad's studio, on a former television lot in suburban Dallas where the show *Walker, Texas Ranger* used to be filmed. Raphe was quiet and polite. He didn't seem at all prone to his father's impassioned political soliloquies. As Glenn started to tell me how Raphe had turned him into an AJR fan, he reached out for his son's hand and patted it in a circle as he spoke about a road trip they had taken together a few years earlier:

> I love driving cross-country with one of my children [at a time] because you get hours and hours with them and nothing to do. And I could not figure my son out. And I knew that he was struggling with something, and I had no idea what. I think we got to the edge of Texas, which is a full day, and he said, "I want to play a song for you. I'm not sure you're gonna like it." It was "Don't Throw Out

My Legos." I'm such a fan of production, you know? I was immediately like, "Wow, this is different and great." I heard the song, and I understood my son. The next song he played for me was "100 Bad Days," and I understood him [more]. I admired him. And honestly, I thank you.

"Legos," about growing up and moving on from your parents' house, and "100 Bad Days," about trying to reframe your misfortune as a wealth of good stories, are older tracks, but they remain fan favorites. We know why these songs are meaningful to listeners who are struggling to navigate life as young adults, because that was exactly us when we released them. But parents tell us they also appreciate the lyrics on a whole different level. They're reminded by "Legos" that they're not the only ones afraid of letting go when a child grows up, and they're grateful to see their kids internalize the "100 Bad Days" message about learning to cope with failure. Hearing this from parents has been hugely helpful to us; it's part of why we played these songs at every stop on our U.S. arena tour in 2024, despite it being five years since their release. At any rate, my brothers and I consider the dual dose of appreciation to be a huge compliment. It reminds us of Pixar, which has always been a major source of creative inspiration for us, thanks to its films' inventiveness, aesthetics, and emotional honesty. The studio behind *Toy Story*, *Up*, and *Inside Out* makes movies that resonate deeply, but differently, with kids and adults.

Glenn's connection to AJR's music was making more sense to me now. And meeting him together with his son foreshadowed an important element of AJR's future audience growth. We kicked off our 2024 U.S. tour about six weeks after my trip to Texas. For these shows, we sold an average of 2.7 tickets per transaction, versus the more typical 2.4 tickets per transaction for concerts overall, according to Ticketmaster's parent company Live Nation Entertainment. This (alongside other demographic data) indicated that we were attracting a lot more parents purchasing tickets with the intention of attending with their children. Sure enough, every night, in cities across the country, we played in arenas packed with families, sometimes spanning three generations.

It turns out Glenn and his children share an affinity for several pop and alt-rock artists. But he often hasn't felt comfortable going to concerts with his kids. He knows how polarizing a figure he is. Especially when he was on Fox News every night, outings in public tended to bring out either adoration or hatred from the people who recognized him, he told me.

> When I was in New York, I wanted to see Lady Gaga with my daughter—no way. I wanted to see Muse— no way. Because I just know there are too many people there who would look at me and go: "That guy." And it's just not worth it.

Glenn said he wasn't worried about attending the AJR concert he took his family to in 2022. Maybe that's because he had been largely removed from mainstream airwaves for more than a decade by then. Or because we were playing on his adopted home turf of Texas, where his politics aren't as out of step with popular opinion as they would be in New York. But Glenn also told me our lyrics raised honest, thoughtful questions—"You do it the right way. I've done it the wrong way for a very long time," he said—and he felt this suggested we appealed to a particularly thoughtful audience.

While I take pride in that assessment of our fans, I suspect it's likely at least some of them wouldn't be very welcoming of Glenn, who opposes women's reproductive rights, sees the influx of migrants to the United States as a "global invasion," and once argued that supporting trans rights is a gateway to acceptance of pedophilia. But until I came to understand what it was about our music that specifically appealed to him, I would have thought it even less likely that Glenn would be an AJR fan in the first place. Had he heard our song "Birthday Party," in which we muse about living in a country that's nice to immigrants? Was he aware I had met with members of the Biden administration and lobbied Congress to pass the Inflation Reduction Act, the transformative law that Glenn described to his audience as a "war on American energy"?[2] He had, and he was. And apparently it made him no less admiring of "God Is Really Real" (another song he mentioned to me by name over the course of our wide-ranging dialogue covering music, politics, history, philosophy, religion, family, and climate science), and it certainly didn't seem to make him any less appreciative of how our music connected with his teenage son during a challenging time.

And that brings me to the other reason I went to see Glenn. I had requested the meeting primarily because his tweet made me realize I didn't know my audience as well as I thought I did. But also, I wanted to test my faith that civil debate can be had with anyone once you find common ground.

HOW BIG A TENT?

In a political environment that's growing more divisive by the day, it's easy for anyone growing a fan base—whether a band, a brand, or a movement—to decide at the outset who they *won't* appeal to, if only to help focus their growth efforts elsewhere. But when you're trying to reach critical mass, it doesn't make sense to needlessly narrow the scope of your potential audience, even at the margins. That's not to say you have to make friends with everyone. And certainly you shouldn't compromise your values or tactics for the sake of appealing to a wider audience than you intended. You just need to be crystal clear about what your values and tactics are, and let your potential supporters decide whether this is a fan base they want to align themselves with, instead of doing the sorting-out for them. You might be surprised by who opts in.

Inviting diverse participation is great because it attracts new perspectives that can help erase blind spots and stoke creativity. But in a heavily divided society, it sometimes raises conflicts. Can someone who drastically opposes you on one issue stand with you on another? Or are some positions indefensible to the point that they negate the person's contributions to discourse entirely? It's sort of like having to decide whether you should sit through another Thanksgiving dinner with your retrograde relatives or skip out on the whole gathering. Maybe there's no "right" answer that fits all circumstances. But each choice ensures a different outcome: One has you sitting around the holiday table with family, and the other doesn't.

In the push for social change, sometimes sitting at the table with the opposition is the only way to get something done. Even then, success isn't guaranteed. But when the strategy works, the result can be very meaningful.

COULD YOU HAVE THIS KIND OF PATIENCE?

In June 2022, Congress broke a decades-long stalemate on serious gun reform to pass the Bipartisan Safer Communities Act, America's first substantial gun safety law in nearly thirty years. It expanded background checks for gun buyers under age twenty-one; funded programs for mental health, school security, and crisis intervention;

and closed a huge loophole in rules meant to keep guns out of the hands of people convicted of domestic violence crimes.

John Cornyn led the charge to get his fellow Republicans to support the bill. The Texas senator had always been a hard-liner on guns, with an A+ rating from the National Rifle Association. But after a mass shooting at Robb Elementary School in Uvalde, Texas, which killed nineteen students and two teachers, Cornyn was ready to get something done. One of the interest groups he opened his door to was Sandy Hook Promise, whose storytelling strategies we examined in Chapter Three. Nine years earlier, the parents of Sandy Hook Promise had been devastated when the Senate failed to pass a background checks bill proposed after the shooting at the Sandy Hook Elementary School. Only four Republicans had supported that bill, and Cornyn wasn't one of them.[3] But the group worked with his office a few years later on a bill to expand access to mental health services. (That bill, passed in 2016, was a way of addressing a key factor in school gun violence without cornering Republicans like Cornyn into publicly acknowledging America's gun problem.) With that trust established, Sandy Hook Promise worked with Cornyn once again after Uvalde, even helping to draft language in the bill that passed in 2022.[4]

Little in this patient approach to relationship-building came naturally to Mark Barden, at first. A career musician who played in bands and gave guitar lessons, Mark helped start Sandy Hook Promise after the shooting death of his seven-year-old son, Daniel, in a classroom at Sandy Hook Elementary. Having grown up in a household where even cap guns and water pistols weren't allowed, Mark had never understood gun culture. Now he was seething at it. But whatever his feelings about America's gun problem and the terrible way in which it affected his family, Mark learned to not let his in-

stinctual anger steer him off course as he spearheaded legislative affairs for Sandy Hook Promise. If getting enhanced background
checks, school safety funding, and crisis-intervention programs
would require working with Second Amendment defenders who
needed the cover of a mental health bill to start addressing America's gun problem, then that's what he would do. It sounds like a lot
to ask of a father still openly grieving the loss of the son he refers to
as "my little Daniel." But as Mark explained to me:

> One of our consultants told me early on: "We're not here
> to fight; we're here to win"—because I was ready to fight
> everybody, always. And she said, "This is going to be
> really hard. It's going to take a lot of time. But you're
> talking about social change. You're talking about chang-
> ing people's attitudes and behaviors. You're talking about
> movement-building. And all of those things take a lot of
> time."

The consultant was right. After the gut punch of watching the Senate vote down the background checks bill written in response to the
shooting in their own community, Sandy Hook Promise—and the
rest of the country—waited nearly a decade for the Senate to finally gather enough Republican support to pass a gun safety law.
The Democrats were ultimately joined by fifteen Republican senators, five more than were needed to break the stalemate, while in
the House, fourteen Republican members voted with the decisive
Democratic majority.[5] Though the law was hardly a comprehen-
sive response to America's gun violence epidemic, the somewhat
bipartisan vote at least suggested that momentum on the issue was
gathering.

THE SEMI-SPIRITUAL VIRTUE OF POLITICAL MATH

Political math has bearing on all kinds of social change, of course, but it can feel brutally disconnected from the moral imperatives that drive movements. It's a purely practical consideration that places no value on passion or principle; it leaves little room for anger, resentment, or mistrust of those on the other side of an issue; and it constantly threatens to undermine hope. Yet there is also a certain grace to be found in it, as longtime activist Jamie Drummond pointed out to me. A London-based veteran of activist campaigns addressing global health and poverty, Jamie saw America's bifurcated political scene up close while partnering with U2's Bono on African relief issues, starting in the late 1990s.

It was Jamie who had recruited the Irish rock star to join Jubilee 2000, an international campaign to wipe out tens of billions of dollars in debt owed by the world's poorest nations. Then they worked together on securing a massive commitment from the United States to address the African AIDS crisis, and later they co-founded the ONE Campaign.

Bono, politically on the left and among the most popular musicians in the world at that point, needed the support of powerful religious-right conservatives in the U.S. government who were not initially on board with debt forgiveness or meaningful AIDS funding. Both times, the rock star brought not only his statistics and arguments, but also his religious faith, into the conversation. Using the common ground of their shared Christian values, and invoking a sense of biblical purpose in his mission to help the world's poor, Bono won the backing he sought from the religious right in Congress and in the George W. Bush White House, resulting in billions of dollars of debt forgiveness for Africa during the Clinton administration, and billions more in assistance from the Bush administration to fight the AIDS crisis.

According to Bono, who recounted the achievements in his autobiography, the bipartisan politicking jeopardized several of his friendships and exasperated his bandmates. Meetings with Republican Jesse Helms, a rabidly homophobic senator from North Carolina who was also famously ungenerous with foreign aid, proved especially polarizing within the musician's camp.[6] But even Jamie, described in Bono's memoir as having a certain "moral indignation,"[7] saw the appeal of maintaining a big-tent approach. After all, lobbying by conservative evangelicals helped convince Bush in 2003 to create what *New York Times* columnist (and longtime Bush critic) Nicholas Kristof has called "the most important humanitarian program in American history." The President's Emergency Plan for AIDS Relief, or PEPFAR, is credited with saving an estimated twenty-five million lives in its first twenty years.[8]

Reflecting two decades later on the policy victories he helped secure from behind the scenes, Jamie said this when I asked him about the lessons he took from the experience:

> There's a semi-spiritual thing about redemption and grace and the belief that you can and must try to talk with people, even the ones that you disagree with—partly because sometimes they might be right and you might be wrong, but also because it's usually the synthesis that is the right idea, or the healthiest one, or the one that's most likely to work and get through. That's a point about politics in democracies, but it's also probably a point about human relations more generally, and interethnic, interracial, or intercultural understanding and cooperation.
>
> And it's believing people can change, but also some-

times you're the one that might need to change. We had specific experiences like the famous one with Jesse Helms, but also President Bush and others, where we did a bit of leading them to our side, but they probably also helped us become more of the center than of the Left. And we don't think of the center as a soft place, but as a radical, spiky-edged place that's about getting things done.

Also, "compromise" is not a dirty word. It means two people promising, and that's actually quite beautiful. Obviously there are some things you shouldn't compromise on. But there's plenty that you can, to get something done.

I've predicated my own policy work on very similar sentiments, although I've probably never articulated them as exquisitely as Jamie just did.

HOW I LEARNED TO SPEAK DEMOCRAT AND REPUBLICAN

Climate advocacy has interested me for almost as long as music has, but actually crafting climate policy? That came much later. Ironically, one of the roads that led me there was listening and learning from AJR's audience. For example, there was the young fan from the U.S. Midwest who told me that my advocacy work inspired her to start a campaign to eliminate single-use plastics from her school cafeteria. Next she was hoping to turn her victory into a policy for her entire school district. Then there were fans we met who were already deeply affected by the effects of the Earth's temperature rise, from wildfires in California to record heat in Rome. Fans in these places would be coping with the local consequences of climate change long after we moved on to our next tour stop. Eventually I realized that my job as a musician was informing my work on climate issues, and that whatever platform I had could be put to more productive use not just supporting research and awareness, but actively shaping policies to hasten our much-needed transition away from fossil fuels. But where to begin? I started setting up appointments with members of Congress representing every region of the country.

I won't lie: Having even minor celebrity status can help open a lot of doors in Washington. While this admittedly felt a bit icky to me initially, I knew that once the photo ops were over, the meetings would quickly pivot to substantive discussion in which my music career would matter far less than my credentials on climate issues. I can get plenty technical when the conversation calls for it. But even more than talking in these meetings, I wanted to listen. This was another audience I really wanted to get to know. To achieve something meaningful, I would need to understand what concerned them, how to best connect with them, and where there was enough common ground between them to turn a policy proposal into reality.

Many of the Democrats I met with talked about their interest in *renewable energy, environmental justice,* and *carbon reduction.* The Republicans had an entirely different vocabulary, focused on terms like *clean energy* (as opposed to renewable), *energy security,* and *conservation.* And both sides were equally fluent in the language of jobs for their districts. It didn't take long to see that *energy development* and *strategic land use* would speak to all of their interests. The policy we pitched, aptly named Common Grounds, involves co-locating renewable energy projects on eighteen million acres of federal land that has already been leased to oil and gas companies, largely in the American West.

In an interesting plot twist, we heard some of the strongest pushback from environmental and wildlife protection groups, several of which were opposed to the construction of wind and solar farms. This was a good reminder that when you're pushing for climate action—or global health funding, gun regulation, education reform, racial justice, gender equality, or anything else that falls under the realm of social progress—you aren't working in a vacuum. You're part of a larger cause, and that cause is likely to include people or groups with very different tactics or priorities from yours. I knew that everyone in this particular debate was interested in restoring and protecting the health of the planet. But some drew lines at solutions that they thought could harm species of plants or birds and threaten surrounding ecosystems; others didn't want to see an urgently needed transition to renewable energy slowed down by wildlife concerns. Clean power generation at scale requires massive amounts of land. Could we find a way to support the transition away from fossil fuels without further disturbing nature? We had to find a middle path. And we did.

We ultimately secured the blessing of key environmental groups and got dozens of senators and representatives, on both sides of the aisle, to pledge their support for the Common Grounds concept. John Curtis, who founded the Conservative Climate Caucus as a House Republican from Utah (he's now a senator), and Mike Levin, a Democrat from California on the House Natural Resources Committee, took the lead and jointly endorsed the proposal in a letter to the Department of the Interior.

In 2024, the DOI's Bureau of Land Management signaled its approval of the bipartisan approach, suggesting it would cooperate in authorizing the land for renewable energy use.[9] Operationalizing the idea will take time. But every permit obtained under this proposal holds the promise of jobs that will help develop America's wind and solar energy capabilities, and reduce our reliance on horrendously damaging fuels like oil and natural gas.

PUTTING GLENN TO THE TEST

I told Glenn all about my policy work very early in our conversation at his office that day in Texas. And he shared with me that his second home, a sprawling ranch in Idaho, runs entirely on clean energy— solar, primarily—with natural gas as a backup. But why would someone who saw the wisdom of investing in renewables also oppose the Inflation Reduction Act, the transformative 2022 legislation providing important incentives to wean the U.S. economy off fossil fuels? As Glenn explained it:

> I bought a thousand acres up in this canyon and I want it to remain pristine. I want it to be clean. I treat my animals right. I mean, I do what everybody does if you're a normal, decent human being. . . . I believe global warming and climate change is happening. But the solutions so far are insane, and the fact that the cleanest energy of them all—nuclear—isn't even considered is insanity to me. The fact that we now say natural gas, which is really clean, has got to go away, is insane. To go on to all electric cars without even thinking about the transmission lines—we can't make that much [renewable] energy, nor can we transmit that much energy [to match demand].

We actually were in agreement that the United States is going to need a lot more infrastructure to support its renewable energy transition. But something in his argument really bothered me. A couple more hours into our discussion—after we had established a mutual love of music, a joint desire for healthier public discourse, and a shared interest in religion that developed in adulthood (I did my master's degree in constitutional religious law, and became a Bar

Mitzvah in my thirties; Glenn, a lapsed Catholic, enrolled in a theology class at Yale, and researched a variety of denominations before converting to Mormonism in his thirties)—I finally asked if we could go back to his comment about natural gas being "really clean." Glenn was agreeable. I wanted to know why he said natural gas is a clean source of energy, and what his sources were. "I've always heard that—that it's a clean source and the cleanest that we have," he replied. "I'm not saying it's clean. I'm saying it's clean*er*."

Okay. It was time to debate. I acknowledged that Glenn was correct that natural gas *is* much cleaner than oil in terms of emitting carbon dioxide. But then I explained that it's way worse when it comes to emissions of methane. While methane thankfully doesn't hang out in the atmosphere as long as carbon dioxide does, it has roughly eighty times the warming effect of carbon dioxide while it's up there.[10] So if there's one thing we can do to immediately combat the extreme weather the Earth is experiencing now as a result of climate change, it's to plug the appalling number of gas leaks from natural gas pipelines. That's just a short-run solution, by the way. In the long run, we should be decreasing our use of natural gas with an eye toward phasing it out entirely as we develop the right storage and transmission systems to support wider use of renewable energy sources. I said all of this to Glenn, who quickly responded:

> If that was the message, as opposed to "We're taking away your gas stoves," okay! Fix the leaks, I'm fine with that; and phase it out eventually, I'm for that. But you have to be a complete and total moron to think we can go all-electric [with] cars by 2030 and eliminate all fossil fuels by 2035. It's not possible. Let's set reasonable dates where it's not going to bankrupt everyone, and you're going to have [enough] energy still.

Clearly we didn't have the same debating style, Glenn and I. His high-octane delivery is rooted in his early career as an FM morning-zoo radio host; I quickly go into academic mode and can get a bit lecture-y. But we were inching our way toward another plot of common ground, where at least we could cultivate meaningful conversation. Personally, I think we could have been well on our way toward achieving those timelines Glenn cited, had companies not recently rolled back their climate commitments—although I'm concerned that low-income areas especially will be slow to get access to the infrastructure they'll need for things like charging electric vehicles. So, okay, point partially taken.

There was one other thing I needed to know from Glenn before I left. While partisanship has always been part of national life, it really went off the rails during Glenn's heyday on cable television. The breakdown in discourse has lots of other factors, of course, from the rise of the internet and social media news-feed bubbles, to the increasing concentration of wealth among the richest Americans. But it was Glenn who brought his radio shock-jock antics to television and applied them to a show about politics, setting a troubling new standard for cable "news" shows that are long on invective and short on facts. On Fox, he accused then-president Barack Obama of hating white people. He fantasized about poisoning Nancy Pelosi when she was Speaker of the House.[11] He applied faulty economic logic to suggest in 2010 that the Federal Reserve was courting Weimar Republic–level hyperinflation.[12] One of Glenn's big soapbox issues now is the decline in civil discourse in our country; he wants to help nurse it back to health. But does he take responsibility for its current state? He offered an unflinching answer:

Of course I do.

I was going to have to stop being so surprised by Glenn, who went on to explain how he felt he had erred at the peak of his fame.

> My job was to tell the truth as I understood it. I tried really hard to tell the truth, and I told it in an entertaining way, because the second part of my job is to draw people in. But [the audience] took everything I said seriously. And so the combination of me being stupid, naive, and just trusting that everybody's got the right intention here . . . I made mistakes. I said things I shouldn't have said, just stupid things. You know, that show was live most times without a prompter. And then [I] had three hours of radio on top of that. Yeah, you're damn right I'm gonna say stupid things; of course I am. And I tried to apologize for them. After I woke up, I made sincere apologies to people, in person, to anybody I thought I wronged. But it doesn't . . . you know, you don't go back. You just can't go back.

No, you can't go back. But you can move forward, ideally with the grace that comes from having learned something about yourself and the causes you care about, and also the kind that comes from giving grace to others.

TIPS FOR PITCHING TENTS

In both music and movements, there are a lot of questions to ask yourself as you pitch a tent. So I've established a handful of camping recommendations, based on my meeting with Glenn Beck, my experience running around Congress, and the advice of Mark Barden,

Jamie Drummond, and others who pitch tents that are wide enough to encompass multiple points of view.

1. When you assume, you really do make an "ass out of u and me." Many artists and movements fall into the confirmation-bias trap of believing that their audience is exactly who they want their audience to be. For a long time, we thought it was cool that AJR appealed to college kids, and while many of our fans do sit in the 18-to-24-year-old demographic, we realized that the live show attendance of 8-to-80-year-olds was vital to further developing our fan base.

2. Ask your audience who they are. While Spotify or Instagram will tell us about the age, gender, and location of AJR fans, they can't (or won't) share the more valuable information that may help us better define our audiences. Your music or your cause is useful for attracting fans at first. An audience focus group, or other opportunities where you can speak to fans directly, is more useful for growing. Without talking to him, I never would have known that Republican John Curtis of Utah was open to expanding renewable energy policy.

3. Marketing to a sixty-five-year-old is very different from marketing to a twenty-year-old. Once you know who your audience is (and could be), don't let it change the thing you are doing, but let it inform how you talk about it. Getting Republicans and Democrats to engage on the same energy policy was purely a matter of word choice. (Another benefit of actually speaking to the audience is that it will clue you in as to the type of language that will resonate most strongly.) Or you can poll a larger sample to figure out which words work for which people. Pretend you're running for president and message-test everything!

4. Search for small similarities and save the debate for later. If you

start conversations firmly on one side or the other, you'll inevitably alienate some of the people you may want as part of the audience. As trifling as it may seem, begin with the nuance. Finding one small part of the issue where there is room for agreement, even if it feels meaningless on a big scale, will open the door to progress.

5. Time is your friend, so stop racing against it. When you are in the streets marching, or getting angry about something you see on the news, you may get frustrated or upset about the system. "I don't understand why we can't just stop using fossil fuels!" Everything takes time. Our problems are urgent and it's natural to feel impatient, but if you are in for systems change, you have to understand that you will be in for the long haul. The eighteen months it took Planet Reimagined just to get approval to start lining up renewable energy projects on oil and gas leases was incredibly fast for Washington, D.C. Change is a grind. Even my hours with Glenn were a grind—a good grind, because we found that moment of agreement that put us on common ground.

FEAT.

CAN FEATURING HELP WITH
THE EXPANSION OF MOVEMENTS?

When my brothers and I started AJR, our goal was to become a successful touring band. We were greatly encouraged when our single "I'm Ready" went platinum in 2015, and felt even more confident a couple of years later when "Weak" exploded on Spotify. None of it was enough. At hometown shows in New York City, we usually drew decent crowds and could always count on a few dozen friends and family members to help fill the room. In most markets, though, we were lucky if we could sell more than a couple dozen tickets per show.

After years of trying, we just weren't getting consistent enough play on Top 40 radio to expand our audience. Our melodies, instrumentation, and orchestrations were more reminiscent of Broadway musicals than anything playing on pop radio at the time, and station programmers were skeptical of our theatrical sound. But everything suddenly changed for us after we released "Sober Up," featuring a bridge by Rivers Cuomo, the front man for the alt-rock band Weezer.

Rivers was a fan of our song "Weak," and we had connected with him after he tweeted about it. A collaboration soon followed. On "Sober Up (feat. Rivers Cuomo)," that's Rivers singing the melodic bridge he wrote, which begins: "My favorite color is you / You're vibrating at my frequency." The song, which would eventually become a staple of our shows, did nothing initially to help our stature in the pop world. It did, however, catch the attention of a radio programmer at an alternative music station in Denver, probably thanks to Rivers's involvement. Immediately, there was a spike in Shazam activity in Denver, from people using the app to identify the track. Our manager, Steve Greenberg, took one look at the data and advised us on a new strategy. After struggling for so long to build an audience for our genre-fluid music by tying ourselves to mainstream pop, it was time to change course. We were going alternative.

This might not sound like a big deal. But it hadn't been tried in pop music before. While plenty of acts over the years had crossed over from alt to pop, we knew of no examples of the shift ever happening in reverse. Streaming services like Spotify have done a lot in recent years to break down the barriers between genres. But in radio, these silos still mean something. Pop bands are marketed to pop stations, and alt bands to alt stations; you pick one lane or the other, and you don't duplicate campaigns promoting the music. Sure, at the time there were bands playing on both types of stations simultaneously, including Imagine Dragons, Panic! at the Disco, and Twenty One Pilots. But our music went further out on the pop spectrum than any of those acts. Steve's industry friends, including heads of major record labels, warned him that trying to change course and pushing us to alt stations was crazy enough to hurt our reputation with both formats, not to mention his own credibility, but he couldn't be dissuaded. That's just kind of how Steve is. And considering how elusive success had been for us at that point, the band really didn't have much to lose.

After running into a wall of skepticism, Steve finally found a radio promoter who was willing to help us try to get the song some alt-radio airplay in a second market, just to prove that what had happened in Denver wasn't a fluke. Fortunately, a station in Buffalo, New York, gave the song a chance. Once again, "Sober Up" exploded on Shazam, this time from users in Buffalo. We soon replicated this success in market after market, as alt stations around the country agreed to play the song. As Steve recalled:

> The song went to number one on alternative radio, and it really changed the trajectory of AJR's career, because all of a sudden, AJR realized, "Oh, our music actually is being embraced in the alternative music community." So it was good that we tried, because if we hadn't tried, we never would have known that.

Our move into alt radio and our recategorization as "alt pop" had all kinds of positive ripple effects for us. With our stuff getting played alongside music from bands like Walk the Moon and Foster the People, we started getting offers to play at festivals like Lollapalooza and Bonnaroo. And our experiences with radio station interviews instantly improved. Whereas the pure pop stations were mainly interested in knowing things like who was the messiest brother, the alt DJs actually wanted to talk about the music and our shows. Most important, we quickly began growing our live fan base. We finally had the traction we had been looking for, and it began with the decision to feature Rivers and his anthemic bridge on "Sober Up."

Featuring is, in fact, a commonly used tactic in the music industry to help artists reach beyond their existing fan base. The strategy has become especially important with the rise of solo artists, who almost completely rule music now.[1] The ascendance of solo acts versus groups makes sense given how much of the industry now revolves around social media, where it's far easier to convey the personality of an individual artist than an entire band. But consider this: While bands contributed just four tracks to the 2023 year-end Billboard Hot 100, with the rest credited to solo artists, a full thirty-one songs on the chart that year featured more than one singer.[2]

Collaborations are basically the standard now. Often, they bring together artists from different genres. In 2023, for example, Afrobeats star Rema and American pop star Selena Gomez teamed up on "Calm Down," while dance/electronic DJ David Guetta and pop's Bebe Rexha came together for "I'm Good (Blue)." Both pairings yielded Top 10 hits.[3] But even collaborations within a single genre, whether pop, hip-hop, Latin, or country, can powerfully fuse fan bases together and provide artists an excuse to effectively re-release their work to their existing fan base, giving them a second shot at having a hit.

THE UNTAPPED POTENTIAL FOR MOVEMENTS

In social activism, it's not unusual for like-minded organizations to come together to advocate for a shared policy goal or a mutually preferred political candidate. (Sometimes allies don't even have to be that like-minded, as we saw in the previous chapter.) But it's always been surprising to me that movements don't do more to coordinate across different causes—not even necessarily in service of a shared goal, but simply to tap into one another's audiences as a routine way of reaching new pools of potential supporters.

Most of us live lives that are impacted by multiple issues at any given time. And many of us have the capacity to care deeply about more than one issue simultaneously. It's true that you can't count on everyone who supports climate action to also support trans rights or drug legalization, and not everyone who supports gun control also supports abortion access or unionized labor. But wouldn't it make sense for social action groups to regularly wade into one another's worlds, to borrow from one another's support systems and strategically cross-pollinate their ideas with people who are demonstrably passionate about one issue and might easily be counted upon to support another? It doesn't happen more often because the movement world is largely siloed, just like radio with its pop and alt stations. And that's unfortunate, according to Hahrie Han, a political science professor at Johns Hopkins University who studies organizing and collective action. As she told me:

> The movements that I've seen historically that are the most effective always start with the question of "Who are my people?" and not the question "What is my issue?" When you divide things up into issues, which is how our nonprofit complex is set up, then yes, it's kind of like, "Well, I'm an environment person, so why would I go work over here on this housing thing or on this healthcare thing?" But you [could take the approach of], "Here are my people, and they don't experience climate and housing separately; they just have these different problems that they have to fix in their lives." And when you see organizations that are grounded in a constituency in that way, then they tend to really have a more collaborative approach.

What Hahrie is describing might apply to community service groups or churches. But as she noted, that's not how much of the movement

world has been constructed, especially at the national level. Movements are mainly organized by issue or cause. Sometimes, two or
more movements will come together in pursuit of a shared goal.
Rainforest protection efforts, for example, tend to unite environmentalists and animal rights groups, while tenants' rights campaigns
might join anti-poverty activists with advocates for senior citizens.
And sometimes, seemingly disparate groups bump up against one
another in less expected ways. This often is the result of a backlash
against one group, which then spurs an entirely different group to
take action. For example, when police began violently cracking
down on civil rights demonstrators in the American South in the
1960s, white Catholic clergy in the North began to more actively
frame racial segregation as not just a political issue but a moral injustice.[4] Or, for a more contemporary example, consider the cyber-
revenge campaigns unleashed by the hacker collective Anonymous
against the Church of Scientology in 2008, and Visa and Mastercard
in 2010. The first happened after the Scientologists pressured You-
Tube to pull down a video on questionable grounds, citing copyright violations,[5] and the second happened after the financial giants
froze payments to WikiLeaks, the leaked-documents site.[6] In both
cases, the "hacktivists" of Anonymous were acting in response to
what they saw as attempts at internet censorship.

These examples of backlash activism were pointed out to me by
Jennifer Earl, a sociology professor at the University of Delaware.
Her work shows that the mash-up of movements can have some
really interesting consequences. Jennifer and a research partner,
Misty Ring-Ramirez at Austin Peay State University in Tennessee,
examined decades' worth of evidence showing how movements
form and evolve. And they found proof of what they call "agenda
spillover," which they define as occurring "when the goals of one
movement come to be taken up by another movement in a serious or

enduring manner (e.g., when racial justice goals become embedded in environmental goals)."[7] They argue that successful movements ultimately influence not only the media or politicians or the public at large, but also one another. But even Jennifer agreed with me that movements could be a lot more deliberate about when and how they seek allies from other corners of the movement world.

Political affiliations and demographic data can help point out where likely overlaps in interest already exist, and where there might still be areas with untapped crossover potential. Sites like Change.org nod to this in at least a passive way: Visit a web page about a particular petition on the site, and it will show you a range of other petitions when you scroll to the end, sort of like a shopping site that presents additional merchandise you might be interested in, based on your search activity. But surely there's room for movements to get more proactive in cross-pollinating their ideas and appealing to one another's audiences.

HOW TO COLLAB

Let's say your organization has decided it's time to try branching out, with an assist from another organization. What's the best way to proceed?

Well, in music, collaborations occur in all kinds of ways. An artist picking someone to feature might choose to work with a good friend in the industry, or an artist they've never even met but have always admired, or an up-and-comer they've agreed to help out, whether out of genuine mentorship or simply because they have the same manager or record label. They might be doing it for the creative spark that can come from a collaboration, or for the chance to ride someone else's coattails. A clever, well-timed collaboration can have the power to pull a fading artist back from the brink of obscurity and give them fresh relevance; it also can help a still-popular artist move their sound (or image) in a whole new direction.

Sometimes the featured artist is given explicit instructions about what to sing and how to sing it, or they might be given complete freedom in coming up with their contribution. Some songs are recorded as a "featuring" track at the outset; other times, a guest artist is invited to create a new version of a song that's been previously released. A lot of fans might be disappointed to know that a "feature" doesn't necessarily indicate that the artists were bonding in person at the recording studio. Often a featured artist's contribution is recorded elsewhere and dropped in. Sometimes the artists never even meet.

In short, there are no limits to how a "feature" arrangement can be structured. Social change organizations, too, can be flexible and inventive in designing cross-movement collaborations that work for them. Regardless of how the pairings come together, there are two important guidelines that can be easily borrowed from best (if not always followed) practices in the music industry, to help ensure both parties get the most out of the arrangement.

1. Look for a natural fit

"Lights Down Low" singer Max Schneider, or "MAX" as he's known professionally, was thrilled in 2019 when his songs began appearing on playlists made by Suga, a member of the K-pop phenomenon BTS. When Max went to South Korea in January 2020 to play his first show in Seoul, his team helped arrange a meeting of the two musicians at the offices of BTS's label, Big Hit Entertainment. The two hit it off. As Max recalled:

> We just hung out and we got along really well. We're both obsessed with basketball—his name meant "shooting guard" in Korean. We just connected on a human

level. And then he asked me to be part of his [solo] project. And a lot of times in that situation, I'll just say, you
know, "Do you want to swap? Would you like to be part
of one of my songs?"

Max was no stranger to collaborations. He had already worked with
artists ranging from pop singer Hayley Kiyoko, to rapper Lil Uzi
Vert, to Swedish electronic act Galantis.

I don't know how many times I've had Lil Uzi Vert fans
coming to my shows. But that collaboration was authentic, and I adore him, and it was so cool to do it. I try not
to go into [collaborations] thinking [about the crossover
potential]. I try to just go in thinking, *How much do I love
this collaboration and this song?*

I love pop music, and currently Korea and K-pop
music are doing some of my favorite things that I just
connect with. There's a lot of soul in it, there's a lot of
funk, there's a lot of electronic influence.

So, a pairing with a K-pop star already sounded appealing to Max on
multiple levels. In many cases, the goal of featuring is to build crossover appeal, the impact of which can be tricky to quantify even
when it works. But Max knew that at a minimum, working with a
K-pop star would give him broader exposure and a satisfying creative experience.

Just a couple of weeks after their initial meeting, Suga was in Los
Angeles, where Max lives, and the two met up again.

We went to his first basketball game. He had never been
to one, and that surprised me because he was such a pas-

sionate fan. We got to see the Lakers play. And then I sent him a few songs after that. So it happened naturally, but also with intention. I think the meetup is so essential, just to see if you even vibe on a human level.

For me, collaborations have to be organic. I've had one or two in my past that were a little less organic, and those didn't connect the same way. I learned very quickly that if it's not coming from the artists, then it usually doesn't connect with the audience.

A collaboration between Max and Suga would unite two artists from different genres, with distinct fan bases. In the movement world, this would be akin to, say, a collaboration between a literacy campaign focusing on increasing the reading levels of high school students and a climate campaign focusing on combating misinformation. The result could be cacophonous, but with the right framing, it could be an effective way for students to sharpen their reading skills using materials that will help them learn facts about climate change.

2. Let everyone bring something to the project

Originally, Max wasn't sure which of his songs Suga would be interested in collaborating on. He sent him a few to consider. These weren't finished songs, though, which was precisely the point. Sometimes a featured artist is brought in essentially to cover a specific verse or the chorus to a song that is already known and loved by the main artist's audience—Noah Kahan has successfully done this with multiple tracks from his *Stick Season* album, working with Post Malone, Hozier, Kacey Musgraves, Brandi Carlile, and more. But Max was looking for a collaboration that would yield something truly serendipitous. As he explained:

It's not going to be a true collaboration unless both artists feel represented on the song, so I really try my best to leave open as much of the song as I can, and then we can see what feels right together. Sometimes I'll do a bridge or a first verse, or I'll give them the full instrumental and see if they want to tweak it in some way. That's how I like to do it.

With Suga, I sent him a few songs and he chose "Blueberry Eyes." I kept an open second verse, just to see whatever came to him naturally. And then it just really was a trust fall, with him doing his Korean rap that I never would have imagined and now I can't imagine this song without. I love when collaborations bring something out of the song that you couldn't have brought out yourself, where you had to collaborate to create what the song was meant to be.

In September 2020, a few months after Suga released "Burn It (feat. Max)" under his alias of Agust D, Max released "Blueberry Eyes (feat. Suga from BTS)," which at the time of this writing has racked up more than 255 million streams on Spotify.[8] The successful collaboration yielded more opportunities for Max in the K-pop world. He was invited to write for BTS—he co-wrote a track called "Yet to Come"—and has since worked with other K-pop acts, including Huh Yun-jin of Le Sserafim, who featured on his song "Stupid in Love," and the group Tomorrow X Together, which recorded a track Max wrote called "Happily Ever After." The next time Max toured Asia, Yun-jin joined him onstage in Seoul and sang "Stupid in Love" with him, to the unbridled delight of the audience.

You never know exactly where or how far a collaboration will lead you, and sometimes it can take you in directions you never could have expected. But a good pairing always holds the promise of getting you someplace better than you would have gotten to alone.

PUTTING THE PRINCIPLES OF GOOD COLLABORATION INTO (SOCIAL) ACTION

Using Max's collaborative experiences as a guide, how might we go about finding good partners for a featuring arrangement between movements, where the fit makes sense and everyone is invited to contribute something unique? Let's try to imagine it.

Maybe we're an organization on the west coast of Florida, advocating for more resilient infrastructure to cope with climate-related weather events. In that case, it might make sense for us to reach out to activists in the local LGBTQIA+ community, or to parents and educators fighting book bans in Florida schools, as both groups have done a good job organizing residents in the face of difficult odds. We also might want to think through ways to frame the relationship between our campaign and other causes. For example, a study from 2022 found a relationship between above-average temperatures and increased gun violence in a hundred cities across the country.[9] So perhaps there are partners for us to be found from within the gun-reform movement.

We also should be considering the atmosphere we're trying to create with a particular campaign. If we're looking to celebrate a win—say, drawing attention to a provision in federal policy that should help local resiliency efforts—we might want to consult local Pride organizations, which have a lot of experience creating celebratory environments for supporters. How we talk about the issue is also extremely important, so we want to find partners who fit with us from a communication standpoint, especially if the collaboration is going to involve social media. If we examined social media videos and press releases from other activist groups in West Florida, would we find any voices (people of influence) or tones (styles of messaging and video) that are similar to ours, or could at least harmonize with ours? If so, then there may be a fitting collaboration worth exploring.

Building movements is hard work. Why start from scratch if people attached to other causes have already put in the work before you, or could benefit from the work you have already done? A true collaboration should be mutually beneficial, strengthening everyone involved and alleviating the need to duplicate efforts. Finding the right featuring partners is work in and of itself. But I can tell you from experience in both music and campaigns, it's worth it.

FANS WILL SING YOUR PRAISES

Whether in music or in movements, there's a powerful group of cross-pollinators out there that no one really talks enough about, and that's the fans. Even if they're not actively on the hunt to recruit others to the fandom, fans of musicians or causes you care about are probably out there right now, just casually planting seeds with their networks that could yield big things down the line. And now we've seen algorithms that are startlingly good at dispersing those seeds way, way beyond the bounds of traditional follower networks, surfacing content to users who are likely to be receptive to it almost regardless of the content's origins. What I'm referring to, really, is TikTok, which came to dominate the process of music discovery in the early 2020s. And it all started with random TikTok users playing songs in the background of their videos.

At its core, featuring is about collaborating and sharing audiences. How is that any different from what fans do for people and things they're passionate about? In the internet age, user-generated content, or UGC, is the ultimate feature. Many record labels now assess the success of a song based on "creates," which is the number of videos on social media that feature (yes, feature) a song in the background. The video itself could be about anything. Of course, as artists we can try to encourage fans to dance to our music, cook to it, draw to it, do trick shots to it, or any number of things. But this rarely works. (Remember the "World's Smallest Violin" and "The Good Part" examples in Chapter Four? Those songs went viral because other people, not AJR, shared them in videos that connected with audiences.) In the end, we're relying on other people—and the algorithms they're serving—to know their audiences better than we do, and to deliver content that appeals to them, ideally with our music as the soundtrack.

Record label executive Mary Rahmani, who was director of music content and artist partnerships at TikTok from 2018 to late 2020, told me she first recognized the platform's potential for musicians when she would scroll through videos on TikTok's art verticals and notice the songs playing in the background.

> You would find the weird kids, the art kids, and you'd hear the coolest songs, you know? I would Shazam the songs, or I would go old-school and look up the lyrics on the internet, and [the songs would] always come up on YouTube. When I would reach out to the artists, a lot of them would say they'd never heard of the [TikTok] app, but they knew something was happening because they were getting messages from kids and fans—"I heard your song on an app called TikTok"—and they saw a spike in their YouTube views, and also on their DSP [streams].

DSP, or "digital service provider," is industry parlance for music retail or streaming platforms like Spotify or Apple Music. Having been a talent scout for record labels previously, Mary naturally reached out to the artists whose music was blowing up on the app and invited them to meet.

> Many of them didn't have managers or labels. Or, if they did, [these artists] were not a priority. And so I was really speaking directly with the artists and just trying to em-power them—like, "Look, this is a great avenue for you, great exposure, and you should onboard, set up an ac-count, and try to connect and monetize and grow from there." Then eventually it got bigger and bigger and big-ger.

By the time Mary left TikTok, the music industry had been put on notice: Music discovery was now taking place here, and oftentimes the artists themselves didn't have to be involved—although many of them soon would be.

While viral songs on TikTok have been known to emerge on the Billboard Hot 100 chart, the number of trending songs or TikTok followers for a given artist has been no guarantee of their ability to fill seats at live shows. But a single fan, or even just a casual listener who happened to like the fit of a song for a particular video, could now, with the help of a hypersmart algorithm, launch a track into internet ubiquity.

Getting fans to feature your work in their content involves a bit of luck, of course. But it helps when you set the right conditions—namely, creating good work that they want their social media pres-ence associated with, and stepping out of the way so that their content shines. As Mary told me:

I always have to remind labels and managers that artists are not influencers. Their job is to create music and to be artists and to be the avant-garde. In the beginning [of the TikTok era] I would look at artists and tell them, "You can do whatever you want to do. You can be as creative as you want to be. There are no rules." And a lot of them would say, "Well, we're looking at the app and we're seeing all this really funny stuff and intricate editing, and we don't know how to do that, and we feel like we have to re-create that." And [I would think], *Absolutely not! You are the exception to the rule because you are the artist. So your content should be looked at as something that has people connecting with you on a personality level, not as you trying to fit in.*

The app eventually changed a lot. Now you're hearing so much congestion with music and sounds—just random things that users like because it could pair with their content ideation. Do they really care about what they're using? Well, they're not music supervisors. But I think there was a time when you were seeing that level of thoughtfulness put into video creation. Then it became so massive that it just became a lot of noise. [So today] I tell artists: "You need to have a presence on these platforms. But you get to be in charge of what that promotion looks like. It doesn't have to be cheesy or forced, and you can connect in any way that you want to."

Movements, too, have fans on these platforms who know their work and want to post about it in creative and impactful ways. These fans are featuring the movements, in other words, potentially helping them gain exposure to new audiences. It's another form of the hurricane model we examined in Chapter Four, as existing supporters bring new fans into the fold. Movement organizers will want to be in these places to ensure the newcomers are then properly equipped to go back out and reach even more people. Yes, there's a chance that the algorithms won't fully cooperate, and the content from the fans won't be widely disseminated. Going viral always seems to involve an element of luck. But by showing up on these platforms and engaging with their fans there, organizers can create some of their own luck.

PORTRAIT OF THE CELEBRITY AS AN AUDIENCE CONDUIT

If you want to get your movement's message in front of a wider audience than the one you enjoy currently, then perhaps you've considered teaming up with a trusted messenger (an important role we explored in Chapter Two) who comes to the table with their own built-in fan base. This messenger might even be a musician.

I resisted mentioning this not-uncommon strategy until now so as not to confuse anyone; the point of this book, and this chapter specifically, isn't that music or musicians can help amplify movements, but that the tactics used in the music industry to find and engage new fans can be replicated by movements seeking to amplify their message. Moreover, the mixing of music and movements is nothing new. Musicians have been lending their platforms to movements for as long as movements have existed. But the way in which they do it has changed tremendously, especially over the last few decades. In the 1960s, when many popular musicians were aligned with the Vietnam War protesters, anti-war sentiments showed up in the music itself. The messaging today tends not to be so on the nose. And there are other ways in which artist advocacy has evolved over the decades.

The pressures of social media and the generational values of

Gen Z and millennials who are deeply interested in social justice practically demand that artists align themselves with a cause now. In theory, this increases the risk of encouraging celebrity engagement that feels perfunctory and performative, and there's certainly a lot of that to go around. But it turns out that social media is pretty effective at self-regulating smugness when it comes to this stuff. Posts that are less than authentic are frequently sniffed out and scrutinized; haters and even fans will not hesitate to criticize artists who engage with movements in superficial ways. While that might sound off-putting, the good news for movements is that the public can help deter or weed out celebrity-advocacy relationships that could just end up embarrassing everyone involved.

More good news: Many of today's big artists are genuinely conscious of the value of steering fans to experts in the issues they're drawing attention to, and involving local organizations (or featuring them, you might say) in the process. That's a marked change from the 1980s, which were full of splashy efforts by musicians to take part in global awareness campaigns, often revolving around crises many miles from home, often with little sense that they had done their homework on the issues. The biggest acts of the era performed at concerts for human rights and famine relief. They formed supergroups to record megahit charity singles like "We Are the World" and "Do They Know It's Christmas?" The latter especially, with its paternalistic perspective suggesting the entire continent of Africa needs saving by outsiders, is widely recognized today for being "clumsy, patronising and wrong in so many ways," as the newspaper *The Guardian* once put it.[10] Thankfully, the industry has largely moved on from this approach.

Now artists are routinely highlighting the work of local organizations, even when the issues they're tackling are of national or international importance. At U.S. stops during her GUTS World

Tour, Olivia Rodrigo donated a portion of her ticket sales to local abortion groups and invited local chapters of the National Network of Abortion Funds to engage with fans on-site. Noah Kahan has taken a similar approach with mental health, steering concertgoers to resources and advocacy groups in their own cities, while discussing the topic more broadly (and getting granular about his own experiences) during shows and in press interviews. And Billie Eilish has invited both local and national climate groups to engage with fans at her concerts. On her recent tours, she gave small grants to dozens of nonprofits to participate in an "Eco-Village" set up at every show, where featured organizations could share information about their climate work and talk to concertgoers about how to get involved.

The beneficiaries of this attention have responsibilities, too. Local groups invited to engage with a captive audience at a concert have to show up with more than just a fundraising appeal if they want to take full advantage of the exposure. They need to make concrete calls to action, whether that's getting concertgoers to support a petition, asking them to share any provided information with friends and family, or having them sign up for specific actions or events in the future. I promise, the concertgoers will respond.

"But Adam," you say, "anecdotes aren't enough. Show us the data on how music fans really feel about their encounters with activism at the concert arena." Okay, gladly. In 2024, AJR concertgoers took more than 35,000 actions—signing petitions, calling elected officials at all levels of government, checking their voter registration status, signing up to volunteer for local nonprofits, and so on. And that was during just a six-week leg of our U.S. tour! The effort confirmed what my Planet Reimagined colleagues and I suspected after polling concertgoers in 2023 and 2024. With some help from partners, Ticketmaster among them, we had sent online surveys to 350,000 live music fans and conducted sixty-five in-person interviews at various shows, including The 1975 concert in Seattle and iHeartRadio's Jingle Ball concerts in Los Angeles and Miami. A full 70 percent of the survey respondents indicated they had no problem with artists using their platform to address climate change, including 53 percent who felt artists *should* be using their platforms for these purposes. Among fans interviewed in person at the live shows, 78 percent said they agreed artists should speak out on climate change, whether by sharing information about reductions in waste and emissions produced by their tours or by inviting fans to join them in action. And 76 percent agreed they and other fans would likely take climate action if their favorite artists asked them to.[11]

In other words, the era of "shut up and sing" is over, at least when it comes to climate issues, which was the focus of this particular study.

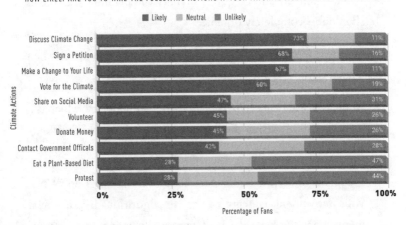

LIKELIHOOD TO TAKE CLIMATE ACTION

HOW LIKELY ARE YOU TO TAKE THE FOLLOWING ACTIONS IF YOUR FAVORITE MUSIC ARTIST ASKED YOU TO?

■ Likely ■ Neutral ■ Unlikely

Movement leaders, take note. The on-site research indicated that direct, personal messaging from the stage, either in pre-show videos or in banter between songs, was ten times more effective than passive signage posted at the arenas. (We tested this at the AJR shows, where fans were spurred on by video messages, arena signage, and volunteers stationed at tables along the concourse.) So if you find an artist interested in spreading the word about your cause, feel free to share this data and let them know that some endorsement methods work better than others. The bottom line is, the fans are ready for it. And once you get them involved, you create a real chance for further momentum. In a follow-up survey of roughly 400 fans who took action at an AJR show in 2024, 82% said they were now interested in learning more ways to make a difference on climate change.

TAKEAWAYS

What should movements keep in mind as they harness the power of featuring?

- A smart collaboration requires strategy and planning, but the fit should feel completely organic.

- It's great when a collaboration feels right, and even better when what's right feels unexpected.

- Audiences today are hypersensitive to inauthenticity, which is a helpful way of raising the bar on collaborations and their outcomes.

- Platforms understand audiences better than humans do. When your movement is featured on an algorithm-driven social media app, the message isn't necessarily going just to your movement's followers. You're being steered through a much broader audience and picking up new fans along the way.

- At the end of the day, keeping genres (or social change movements) in silos is silly, especially when the silos don't neatly encapsulate the work. AJR was in the wrong neighborhood when we were trying to break into pop, and we finally found a home in the alt community. But go figure—when "Bang!" (our highest-charting song to date) took home a Billboard Music Award in 2021, it was for best rock song.

10

"IF YOU WANNA ROCK, YOU GOTTA BREAK THE RULES"

BREAK WITH CONVENTION, DESIGN NEW NORMS, AND CREATE CHANGE ON YOUR OWN TERMS

A little-known fact about me: When I was a kid, I auditioned for the role of Zack, the shy, uptight, guitar-playing fifth grader in the 2003 film *School of Rock*. After three callbacks, I was put "on hold," meaning the casting team was interested enough that they didn't want me taking other jobs that might conflict with their shooting schedule. In the end they chose another Zack, although they never officially told my agent I'd been released from the hold. So technically, I'm still up for the part.

Despite not being cast, I loved *School of Rock*. Unlike most music-themed movies, especially the biopics, it gets its emotional punch from the relationship that any of us can have with music, versus the idiosyncratic and often dramatic backstories of artists themselves. Plus, Jack Black is hilarious as Dewey, the deeply unqualified substitute teacher who ends up dispensing all kinds of wisdom to his students.

While I was growing up, a lot of dialogue from the film got repeated in our family and became inside jokes for us. Other lines took on new resonance as I got older. Dewey's lyric about losing his band ("In his heart he knew / the artist must be true / but the legend of the rent / was way past due") sums up the years when AJR was seriously struggling to get anywhere. What helped the band finally get traction was an idea captured neatly in another line from Dewey: "If you wanna rock," he told his students, "you gotta break the rules."[1]

As musicians go, my brothers and I don't come across much as rule-breakers. We don't trash hotel rooms, get in trouble with drugs, or show up late for gigs. But on a few pivotal occasions, against the advice of people older and wiser than us, we purposely broke unwritten rules of the music industry when they just didn't make sense to us, and we've never regretted it. That's what social movements do, too. They find rules worth breaking in service to a cause, and ambitiously dream up new and improved rules and norms for society to implement.

SEEING AN OPENING

In 2016, AJR served as the opening act for singer-songwriter Ingrid Michaelson, playing for 1,500 to 3,000 people per night. We had never played in venues that big before, and we never would have refused that kind of exposure. But we had been an opener many times before; we knew how this was likely to go.

The main hope of any opening act is that the audience will remember them and buy tickets when the band comes through town again on their own headline tour. That's supposed to be the payoff for going onstage night after night and awkwardly putting yourself between a big crowd of people and the artist they've actually come to see. But it never seemed to pay off for us. Even in cities where our opening set went great and we felt the audience get behind us, we would be lucky to sell fifty to a hundred tickets when we returned to town for a headline show.

A few key concepts from business classes I took in college helped me diagnose the problem—namely, that the whole setup lacked any sense of urgency, scarcity, or connection that would compel a person to take action after seeing our opening set, even if they were genuinely impressed and ready to join our fan base.

So, when we toured with Ingrid Michaelson, I tossed out the industry playbook. No longer would we rely on people to remember us and buy tickets a few months later when the next tour got announced. Instead, in every city where we would soon be playing our own headline show (in a much smaller venue), we announced onstage that tickets for our return date to the area had just gone on sale.

We did this in about thirty markets, which was a nightmare for our booking agent and our marketing team. They essentially had to arrange thirty tour announcements over the course of two months instead of doing everything in one fell swoop, with all of the locations listed and the tickets put on sale at the same time, as is common practice. They weren't happy with me. I didn't care. Right after we played "Weak," at the time our most recognizable song and an emotional high point of the opening set, we made our announcement. Then we would play one last song and watch as Ingrid's fans who had taken to our music would pull out their phones and buy tickets on the spot. That gave us the momentum we needed to sell out our next tour, when we played for crowds four times larger than on our previous headline tour.

I took two important lessons away from the experience. First, getting people to take action means not only appealing to people's emotions but instigating a deeper level of commitment. Second, succeeding at that (whether it's trying to get people to buy a concert ticket, sign a petition, or donate to a cause) requires having systems that are based on the right needs and designed with the right incentives—or developing clever work-arounds when they're not.

While there were no literal rules harmed in the making of our ticketing strategy, we rejected an axiom of the industry, ignored the conventional wisdom of experts on our team, and abandoned the idea that following standard practice was the best way to get where we wanted to go. When we finally ditch obsolete norms, arbitrary conventions, or long-standing problems that we've passively accepted as our reality, we aren't just breaking the "rules"—we're creating a real opening for progress.

THE SECOND TIME WE BROKE THE RULES

The success we had with our new ticketing strategy led almost immediately to our next act of upending industry norms. The venues for that upcoming headline tour had capacities of 200 to 500 people. But the staging we designed was more in line with what bands would spend on shows for 1,000 people. We couldn't help it. We were hell-bent on having light-up drumsticks, which we played on buckets held by fans in the front row, and we insisted on traveling with a stage backdrop that looked like an oversized replica of our sample machine. As our budget climbed way above industry norms for a tour our size, I tuned out a lot of the nay-saying. My brother Jack's memory of it is a lot more visceral, though, so you'll probably find this part of the story more interesting coming from him:

> We got yelled at so much. Every single person we worked
> with said, "This is a terrible idea. What are you doing?"
> And we said, "Guys, we really think this is going to work.
> We think that this is how fans come back." I mean, if we

put on a show, and they go, "Whoa, wait a sec, hold on, I've been to the House of Blues in Dallas a million times and I haven't seen the lights do that," and they tell one friend—and we just need one—then we're going to double [the audience] next time.

So then we moved up to 500-person venues and the same thing happened. We were like, "We're going to put on a show meant for three thousand people, but in a five-hundred-person room." And we got yelled at again. And that was a scary moment, when your manager is concerned, along with everyone that's supporting you—and they're also veterans of the industry. But sticking to your guns as dumb teenagers . . . that was a good move on our part. I'm proud of us for that, because I think it really worked out.

For the record, I was already twenty-three at the time. Jack was fifteen and Ryan was eighteen, and they indeed were dumb teenagers, but not about this. After being told we were spending too much on a tour that put us in front of roughly 14,000 people, we sold 40,000 tickets for our next tour, which supported our album *The Click*. As the crowds and venue sizes kept growing, the arguments against our strategy got quieter and quieter. In 2022, we played for 350,000 people in the United States on our *OK Orchestra* tour, and we sold over 500,000 tickets during our 2024 U.S. arena tour supporting *The Maybe Man*. Even as the tour budgets got bigger, we continued spending more ambitiously than the industry suggested we should. Though the concerts were less profitable as a result, we've never been sorry about that—because more ambitious shows are a lot more fun to plan and play, and because we doubt we ever could have filled arenas without having given our fans everything we could, even at the small shows we played when we started out.

The lesson here? Choosing an unusual course of action sets you up to meet resistance, but demonstrating meaningful progress will help smooth the path.

STEVE'S GOING TO DO *WHAT*?

While our manager was quick to point out the potentially negative consequences of some of the decisions we made in those days, looking back it's no surprise he ultimately gave us the room we needed to test out our ideas. Steve Greenberg is one of the music industry's great rule-breakers. It's one of the reasons we work with him. (He also knew something about working with sibling trios, having signed both Hanson in the 1990s and the Jonas Brothers a decade later to record deals that launched their careers.)

In 2006, when Steve was president of Columbia Records, he produced the Jonas Brothers' debut album. The video concept for the band's first single violated all kinds of industry norms and caused a lot of hand-wringing at Sony, the owner of Columbia Records. It's a great story, and Steve's a great storyteller, so I'll turn things over to him to share what happened.

> In the early days of MySpace, record companies, as a rule—literally as a rule—did not cooperate with social media. [They opposed] giving their music away for free. And I had this record by the Jonas Brothers, it was their first record and it was called "Mandy." We made a crazy three-part video for it. Everything about this thing was going against the grain. Firstly, the video was presented almost like a mini TV series. There was an opening theme

song and a closing theme song and a "stay tuned for scenes from the next episode" [voiceover]. It was like a little teen soap opera with a cliffhanger [at the end of each installment]. All three of the videos were for the same song, though. So that was already really weird and different; nobody had done that before. But then this guy came to my office and explained that you could make a widget—and I didn't even know what a widget was, this was 2005—but he said you can make a widget and kids could take the widget and put it on their MySpace pages, and that as we released more chapters of the video, the new chapters would appear in the widget. That seems obvious today; that's how the internet works now. But back then it was like, "What?" And then the question was, how do we distribute the widget?

In the MySpace era, there were all these websites where kids would go to get stuff to decorate their MySpace page, like banners or glitter graphics or little things today we probably would call emojis. The most popular one of all was called Whateverlife.com, and it was run by a fifteen-year-old girl in Columbus, Ohio. It had all kinds of stuff, but not music—because no record company would ever license music to MySpace, and certainly no record company would give music to a fifteen-year-old girl from Columbus, Ohio, to put on her website to share for free with everybody. So I'm like: "That's what we're doing. We're gonna put this widget on Whateverlife, and fans will be able to take it and put it on their MySpace page."

The brilliance of this move is not just that it rested on the bleeding edge of an emerging technology, or that it greatly ticked off Steve's

Luddite bosses at Sony (though that did happen, and some of us might consider it an added benefit). Steve was simply testing a clever way to launch a new band he was betting on. His odds of success were arguably improved by the fact that he was simultaneously solving an even bigger problem, if not for society at large then at least for some portion of the MySpace ecosystem, where Steve observed both an unmet need and a way for this new technology to address it. As he reminded me:

> No one had ever heard of the Jonas Brothers at this point. But the thing was, there was no other music on Whateverlife.com or on MySpace that was legal, right? And so kids were just thrilled at the idea of being able to get something to put on their MySpace page that was a music video. Within three weeks, sixty thousand kids had put the widget on their pages, which back then was a very big number, and we had twelve million views of the three videos combined, which again back then was a crazy number. And then the song flew up the chart on MTV's *TRL* countdown without even being on the radio.

TRL, you might remember, stands for *Total Request Live,* a hugely popular MTV show that ran from 1998 to 2008. This was precisely the time frame in which the internet came to overtake radio, and then MTV itself, as a vital source of music discovery. Originally hosted by Carson Daly, *TRL* played the ten most requested music videos of the day, as determined by fans voting by phone or online (though sometimes this was gamed, as Steve will explain in a moment). "Mandy" peaked in the number four spot.[2] Until the Jonas Brothers, no band had acquired that kind of status on *TRL* without having a radio hit first. The system had been upended. But the executives at Sony weren't impressed with the new path to success that Steve had discovered. In fact, they were livid, as Steve recalled:

> They got really mad at me. They accused me of actually hiring a company to do the voting on *TRL*, which is a thing people did back then. But I didn't hire a company to do the voting. What we did is, on the widget, we put a little button that said "Vote here for *TRL*" and it would take them to the *TRL* site to vote. So those were real voters. But [the record executives] didn't believe it could work because they didn't understand it. It sort of hastened the end of my time at the Sony Music Group.

After Steve departed Sony and its Columbia Records division, he started his own label and became AJR's manager. The Jonas Brothers, meanwhile, got dropped by Columbia Records, but they soon found a new home at Disney's Hollywood Records label, where over the next six years they made three albums and became gigantic stars.[3] And that's another good lesson about rule-breaking: Even when it succeeds, it might not work out the way you think it will, especially if the incumbent powers aren't yet able to see the wisdom in it. As Steve concluded from the experience:

> Sometimes you can be too early. But that's the thing about great ideas; you can't always time them.

NAPSTER: THE ORIGINAL DIGITAL-MUSIC WILD CHILD

It's hard to have any serious discussion about rule-breaking in the music business—or the timing of ideas, for that matter—without mentioning Napster. Founded in 1999, the free file-sharing service lasted only three years. But in that time it attracted millions of users (along with a ton of litigation) and upended the record business, seeding the digital music revolution that was effectuated a few years later with the arrival of streaming technology.

Napster co-founders Shawn Fanning and Sean Parker were widely seen as rebels with no regard for copyright law; in 1999, the Recording Industry Association of America sued the company on behalf of every major record label in the country, accusing the up-start of providing a safe haven to online music pirates by promising its users anonymity.[4]

It wasn't just the establishment that objected to Napster. Metal-lica and Dr. Dre, big acts with rebellious streaks of their own, both sued the company the following year. Chuck D of Public Enemy supported Napster, however, writing presciently in an April 2000 op-ed for *The New York Times:* "By exposing people to music, com-panies like Napster are creating new fan interest and establishing a new infrastructure for unknown artists to attract an audience—a new radio for the new millennium."[5] Napster settled with Dre and Metallica,[6] but in July 2001 it had to shut down to comply with a court order. By that time, thanks to Napster and a handful of other file-sharing services it inspired, millions of music fans were already accustomed to consuming music digitally. The subsequent rise of streaming platforms from Pandora, Apple, Amazon, and Spotify would only accelerate the conversion and soon solidify digital's dominance.

What I admire about the Napster story isn't that the company broke the law and compromised the livelihoods of artists. It's that Napster's founders saw a problem—in this case, a lack of ease and reliability in transmitting MP3 music files—and came up with an elegant solution. And in finding a way to match music file owners to music file seekers, Napster prompted all of us in the music industry to question our assumptions about our environment. It was a good reminder that sometimes things that feel fixed are in fact entirely changeable.

PRACTICE MAKES PERFECT

Attempting creative innovation at that scale is a tall order, of course. Astro Teller has more experience with this than most. Astro is a co-founder of Alphabet's X division (formerly known as Google X), a self-described "moonshot factory" tasked with creating break-through technologies to tackle some of the world's biggest problems. Alphabet's Verily life sciences business, Wing drone-delivery service, and Waymo self-driving car company all started as projects at X. The division also has a long list of ambitious ideas that haven't panned out, including attempts at building power-generating kites and a balloon-based internet service. That's just the nature of bold ideas—they often don't work. As Astro noted, if the odds of success were high, then the idea probably wasn't all that ambitious to begin with.

Borrowing that framework, I can't say I regret the time I tried figuring out if we could capture the sound waves from screaming fans at an AJR concert in order to create energy that could power the show. On the advice of several equipment companies, and after I'd done a good amount of my own research into the idea, I finally accepted the infeasibility of it. Those are the breaks; time to move on to whatever crazy notion we could come up with next. But coming up with one bold idea after another is pretty difficult, for most of us.

I asked Astro how he primes himself and others to think more expansively, and he shared a bunch of extremely practical tips, which I've laid out for you at the end of this chapter. For now, just to get a sense of the kind of headspace you might want to get into for this type of thinking, I want to tell you about the line Astro asks his team to cross every day upon arriving at work. Literally, he painted a thick line on the floor of the entryway to their office in Northern California, along with a sign that says YOU MAY NOT CROSS THIS LINE! EVER!!! He did this because he wanted people to get practiced at breaking the rules. That's not to say he's an anarchist. "There are rules to *not* break," he acknowledged. "But most of the rules in our minds are not rules. They're rules like that stupid line on the floor."

BREAKING THE RULES FOR REAL

Movements that take stock of whatever landscape they wish to alter can usually find any number of stupid lines on the floor, the unwritten rules that deserve to be broken. But sometimes movements (or individuals who might end up inspiring a movement) deliberately go further than that, breaking *actual* rules and risking serious consequences.

In the United States, nonviolent political protest is a custom that dates all the way back to the colonists who organized the Boston Tea Party. The tradition carried through to the suffragettes arrested a century later at demonstrations demanding women's voting rights. It extended to the 1960 lunch counter sit-ins in Greensboro, North Carolina, which helped inspire the Civil Rights Movement. It was embodied by the New York City AIDS activists who infiltrated the New York Stock Exchange, St. Patrick's Cathedral, and multiple broadcast news studios to demand a response to a crisis that was rapidly unfolding in the gay community in the 1980s. Decades later came the Occupy Wall Street protests in response to the 2008 economic crisis, and the 2015 "debt strike" by students who refused to repay federal loans they were stranded with when the for-profit Corinthian Colleges shut down in a swirl of scandals over deceptive recruiting and predatory lending practices. (Though far less well-known than the previous examples, the "Corinthian 15" eventually helped secure the largest single loan-discharge ever granted by the U.S. Department of Education, with a total of $5.8 billion in debt forgiveness for more than half a million borrowers[7] caught up in the Corinthian fiasco.)

More recently, we've seen a ramping-up of deliberate rule-breaking in the climate movement, with activists hauled off by police for trespassing at a chemical plant in France; for gluing themselves around the speaker's chair inside the British Parliament; and for blocking the entrance to the Federal Reserve Bank of New York, among other actions around the globe.

I've never gone to jail, and I wouldn't endorse it as an end goal (few serious movement leaders would; rather than a rite of passage, getting arrested should be more about what you're willing to risk in order to make a larger point). But I'm a strong believer in civil disobedience, the more strategic the better. If you want to throw soup at a priceless piece of art hanging in a famous museum, I won't stop you. But to me, that's a waste of good soup. Whose attention have you drawn? What exactly have you changed? Just about anyone can find fifteen minutes of social-media fame with an outlandish stunt. It requires a whole other level of strategy to do something attention-grabbing while maintaining a seat at the table where the issue you care about is being worked out politically, or with input from the private sector. Now, you can argue whether that's a table you even want to be invited to. But I'm convinced these kinds of venues, for better or worse, are usually what's needed to produce sufficient responses to complex societal issues.

One organization that has walked this line since its founding in

2023 is Climate Defiance. Feeling betrayed by political leaders and aiming for mass turnout by similarly angry Americans, the group has embraced radical activism, landing its members in jail on multiple occasions. It has noisily disrupted an array of campaign fundraisers and corporate events, and it famously branded West Virginia senator and former coal executive Joe Manchin a "sick fuck" for blocking key legislative proposals to hasten the transition to clean energy. Yet the group has also made overtures to contribute constructively to federal climate policies. It got a private audience in 2023 with senior White House climate adviser John Podesta, where it pressed for an end to government support of fossil-fuel infrastructure, and it was one of several climate organizations that the Biden administration name-checked in 2024 when it agreed to pause new approvals for liquefied natural gas (LNG) exports.[8] (Though the LNG decision quickly got tied up in the courts, the change in policy was considered a big win for environmental groups when it was announced.)

Climate Defiance's north star is what co-founder Michael Greenberg referred to as "action logic," meaning what the movement does is so closely targeting the thing it wants to change, or the specific decision-maker it wants to influence, that its purpose is apparent to even the most casual of observers. Here's how he explained it to me:

> Perfect action logic would be, you know, you want the bus system to be integrated, so you sit in a seat on the bus. Or you don't want a pipeline to be built, so you put your body in the route of the bulldozer that's trying to build the pipeline. We tend to try to have reasonably good action logic. No shade at the groups that do it differently, but . . . we're a little bit more microtargeted.

So you won't find Climate Defiance activists splattering soup at museums. But you may have seen the video of them at a gender equality awards event featuring the head of oil giant Chevron, whom they accused of poisoning women in communities affected most directly by the company's pollution. Or you might have heard about the campaign event where they asked the Democratic governor of Massachusetts to commit to banning new fossil-fuel projects—and then disrupted the backyard fundraiser when she wouldn't make the pledge. Even the stunt with Manchin, conceived not as a serious bid to influence policy but as an attempt at virality, took the group's complaints about the senator right to the source. I asked Michael about the actions that have been most effective for Climate Defiance. He replied:

> The things that went farthest on social media, it's basically a tie between calling Joe Manchin a sick fuck and telling the CEO of Exxon to eat shit; those each got five million views. Blockading the White House Correspondents' Dinner, that was our biggest, most exciting action. In terms of things that had the biggest carbon impact, I'd say the work we did on LNG exports.

It sounds impressive. But is this kind of work, on the fringes of what most people might consider practical, actually worth it? Well, when I spoke with Michael, he said Climate Defiance was operating on a $500,000 budget. That's about one one-thousandth of the combined recent annual spending of the Sierra Club[9] and the Environmental Defense Fund.[10] Or, as Michael put it:

> Normie work is vastly, vastly, vastly overfunded relative to the more disruptive work that makes a bigger differ-

ence. . . . I think it is reasonable to say that while [the Big Greens] have a budget a thousand times greater than ours, they're not making an impact a thousand times ours.

I'd argue the climate movement needs all of these actors, each attacking the problems from different angles and presenting solutions representing a variety of perspectives. Groups like Climate Defiance and Extinction Rebellion grab headlines and supporters by orchestrating acts of nonviolent civil disobedience. The Sunrise Movement, which has chapters in cities and towns and on college campuses throughout the United States, focuses on political action, directly backing candidates who support renewable energy and other forms of climate action. All of these organizations are quite young (the oldest, Sunrise, started in 2017). On the other end of the spectrum we have established players like the Sierra Club, which was founded in 1892. Sierra and the other so-called Big Greens (Environmental Defense Fund, The Nature Conservancy, and the World Wildlife Fund) conduct their advocacy with the backing of more than twelve million members combined. That's nearly twice the margin of difference in the 2020 popular vote for U.S. president between Joe Biden and Donald Trump—so mobilizing these people can really matter! And of course there are countless other campaigns and advocacy groups that make up the movement, from grassroots organizers at the hyperlocal level to national media outlets that are fully dedicated to covering climate issues.

Though some of these organizations might on occasion find themselves competing for some of the same dollars or public attention, there is ample room for all of them. And the fact that their methods differ is part of what makes them valuable contributors to the cause. Some specialize in pragmatism and diplomacy, others are comfortable with direct confrontation, and still others are willing to go beyond the bounds of normally accepted behavior in the hopes of creating change.

So, what's your appetite for breaking rules? Whatever it is, there should be moral principles at stake, so hopefully you're thinking about more than just the economics of your decision. But that old capitalist maxim still applies: The higher the risk, the higher the potential return.

ASTRO TELLER'S TIPS FOR THINKING RADICALLY AND TAKING MOONSHOTS

Sometimes movements can be well served by thinking small. (What's one thing you want to change? What's one thing you can do to initiate a domino effect that could lead to that change? And so on.) But sometimes it's better to think big. When a movement is starting out, for example, or trying to move off a plateau, an audacious idea can help rally people to the cause. Or when a problem is so complex, and the deadline for solving it is tight, a bold solution might be the only real option. Meeting those moments is no easy task. For practical guidance, consider the advice of Astro, and the lessons he shared from his experience taking moonshots while working at Google.

START WITH THE MAGIC. With enough bright people and unlimited funds, it's pretty likely something extraordinary will happen, Astro says. But perhaps cost is also a factor—that's true even at a company as big as Google. If that's the case, don't make the mistake of starting from a place of efficiency. "You have to start at the magic side of the spectrum and then very slowly find ways to turn up the rigor dials, and start to tighten them in ways that don't remove the creativity and the flow," Astro says. "[Maybe] you can get eighty percent of the rigor and eighty percent of the creativity. You'll lose some on both ends, but if you get the settings right, you can get a lot of both."

TRY A BAD-IDEA BRAINSTORM. "If I say, 'Adam, come to a brainstorm at X,' your first thought when you sit down at the table with these legit super-geniuses is pressure and fear of looking stupid, which absolutely kills your ability to be creative," Astro says. "So [I might] say instead, 'Let's come up with some truly terrible ideas.' " Maybe the problem he wants to solve is climate change, in which case he might pitch the idea of genetically engineering humans to be smaller so that we eat less and require smaller buildings, which would re- duce our carbon footprint. "That is not a good idea," Astro ob- serves. "But if the first few ideas come onto the table in that sort of a way, it switches you from the challenge to sound smart to the chal- lenge to play within the rules of the game and to have the idea be really bad. All of a sudden, all that weight is off your shoulders, and you can be much more creative."

It sounds silly, but Astro swears it works. "No brainstorm I've ever seen that starts this way is still doing bad ideas twenty minutes later," he says. "They just can't help themselves; they drift into good ideas. But starting in that way completely opens up the flood- gates of real creativity and much more out-of-the-box thinking."

TRY AN "IDEA TRANSPLANT" TO DEFINE YOUR STRATEGY. Maybe you admire what Uber or Airbnb did to disrupt the car-service or hotel industries. Want to copy them? Get granular in articulating what exactly you hope to replicate. "You might say, 'Uber or Airbnb noticed that there were these depreciating assets that were radically underused—cars and bedrooms, in these cases. What are some other assets that are sitting out there that are underutilized?' That's just an analogy," Astro says, "but that's another source of good brainstorming."

REFRAME SUCCESS. Let's say a team has an idea for a teleportation device. Early tests look promising, so now the team wants to call up the world's foremost expert on teleportation for a consultation. Before they do that, Astro says, the team needs to reorient its self-worth away from the idea of being "right"—because with exercises in radical innovation, they mostly won't be. Maybe they redefine success as simply having improved the odds of finding a workable solution. Now they're ready to call that outside expert and ask them to punch holes in the idea.

CAREFULLY CONSIDER YOUR DEADLINES. Don't mistake Astro's talk of reframing success, or his general comfort with failure, as a signal that he doesn't care about winning. "I'm obsessed with winning; I just have long time frames," he says. But when the window is short—say, twelve months for a political campaign—the experimental phase of the effort needs to get sharply condensed. If Astro were running that campaign, here's how he says he would do it: "I want us to try a hundred things for the next three or four weeks. Then we're going to work day and night to try to learn what worked about it and why. And then, for the next two to four months, we're going to do the top five things. And then we will have exhausted six of our twelve months and probably made very little progress—or maybe we'll have gotten lucky and made some progress. But at the end of the six months, having done almost no actual good, we will know what the right thing is to spend money on in the last six months, and that will get more done than if we all try to sit around a table and come up with the right answer right now."

And if he had six weeks or six years to come up with a plan for winning? "It's exactly the same process," he says. "You just have to scale it to what your time frame is."

A FINAL NOTE ON RULES IN MUSIC AND MOVEMENTS

I can just imagine how movement leaders might react to some of Astro's suggestions for arriving at answers by embracing the chance of failure. Their organizations generally run on budgets that are too lean to leave much room for research and development, let alone outright misfires. While I would love to see social action groups invest a lot more in testing out the potential of their ideas, spending money they don't have would lead to a whole different kind of rule-breaking that I would not endorse.

Most people think musicians live in an artistic space, free of rules. But there are many rules that govern our art, and when they are broken, they can lead to revolutions in artistic expression. Billy Joel sings in "The Entertainer" about writing a beautiful song, only to have the record company "cut it down to 3:05." He was referring to the condensed song length that radio stations encourage so they can fit more tracks on their playlists. But a handful of exceptions have bypassed this norm to brilliant effect, from Don McLean's enduring rock-and-roll masterpiece "American Pie" from 1971, which clocks in at eight minutes and forty-two seconds, to Adele's arresting 2015 ballad "Hello." Making a rare debut at number one on the Billboard charts, "Hello" (the album version) is just under five minutes long. The song was cut for the airwaves, but even the radio edit still ran for a full four minutes and fifteen seconds. It was art. People loved it. They were moved by it. The length was irrelevant.

Breaking the rules is just as much about embracing the art of the possible as balancing the scientific rightness or wrongness of the rules themselves. That's what leads to creativity. In music, this is how we develop new forms of artistic expression. In movements, it's how we inspire people to take action.

WHERE DO YOU SEE
YOURSELF IN TEN YEARS?

SOME PARTING THOUGHTS ABOUT PLANNING
AND GOAL-SETTING

Being a musician, even a relatively successful one, is not the glamorous life it may seem. I realize this sounds like something only a relatively successful musician would say. But I promise it's true. Even when you're filling arenas with twenty thousand people per evening, you're away from home for months at a time, typically traveling overnight on a tour bus where the narrow, shallow sleeping compartments are stacked three high. You might end up sleeping with your face just inches from the floor of the bus, or inches from the roof, unless you're lucky enough to get a cot sandwiched between the high and low ones. Wherever you end up, you'll have no room to sit up and only a flimsy curtain separating you from the eleven other passengers from your band or touring crew. Oh, and you can't poop on the bus because it's not equipped to handle solid waste, so you have to either hold it for the next destination or hope for a pit stop along the way.

These inconveniences feel all the more dispiriting when you're also losing money on the deal. Touring is wildly expensive. AJR didn't make a penny from it until our third headline tour, six years into our career. Seemingly everyone takes a cut of the revenue—booking agents, concert promoters, venue owners, and so on. The remainder has to cover travel expenses, wages for the crew, and a whole bunch of other hefty line items, each of which further stacks the odds against whatever hope you have left of making a living as a touring act. Plenty of artists would tell you the system feels predatory. But few have argued this as pointedly or as publicly as Clyde Lawrence and Jordan Cohen of Lawrence, a pop-soul group out of New York City.

With their take-home from each show getting split eight ways—Lawrence has two lead vocalists, a drummer, a guitarist, a bassist, and a three-person horn section—these musicians perhaps had special motivation to scrutinize the status quo. Among the questions Clyde and Jordan asked: Did Live Nation Entertainment, the parent company of Ticketmaster and the owner of hundreds of concert venues around the world, really deserve a 20 percent cut of the band's merch sales every night, on top of a fixed fee to use the venue, a fee to market the show, and even a fee for providing clean towels backstage? And could any of those rates, which are typically worked out between the venue and the concert promoter, be trusted to have been negotiated in good faith when Live Nation owned both the venue and the site's exclusive promoter? As Jordan recalled:

> On tour, Clyde and I found ourselves night after night arguing with promoters, asking, "Why is it this way? Like, we all agree, this shouldn't be the way, right?" And the unfortunate soul who was settling the show at the

venue that night would be like, "Yeah, I agree with you. But it's not my job. I'm just here to pay you. I can't do anything about it."

Clyde, who started the band while a student at Brown University, and Jordan, the group's tenor saxophonist and tour manager, would never describe themselves as activists. But they had clearly identified a change they wanted to see in the world, which if you recall from Chapter One is the first step in finding a cause. The pair soon emerged as leaders in a movement of sorts, to make the touring industrial complex friendlier to artists. They helped secure several concessions to that end from Live Nation. And they did so using tactics that, as musicians, would be second nature to them, and which by now should be familiar to you as well. Since we've reached the final chapter of this book, let's review, using Clyde and Jordan's experience as a case study. Then we'll bring back some familiar characters to help close us out.

FIND EFFECTIVE WAYS TO TELL YOUR STORY

In 2022, Ticketmaster drew a tidal wave of attention when it mismanaged the pre-sale for Taylor Swift's blockbuster Eras tour. The worldwide attention on the Taylor Swift ticketing debacle created the perfect opening for Clyde and Jordan to tell their story, despite their concerns being focused on Ticketmaster and Live Nation's treatment of artists, not fans. Clyde laid out his case plainly in an op-ed for *The New York Times,* sharing sample calculations to show how Live Nation was profiting at the expense of artists.[1] The clear, measured piece grabbed the attention of someone in Senator Amy Klobuchar's office, who invited Clyde and Jordan to testify at a

Senate Judiciary Committee hearing on the live entertainment industry.

The stories they told on Capitol Hill also turned out to be effective. As Clyde told me:

> Lo and behold, that parlayed itself into us being able to have some actual sit-down conversations with Live Nation about some of the key issues that we really care about, which I think they realized were a little tangential to these broader antitrust, consumer-facing ticketing issues—which are super important, but just not what Jordan and I had become experts in. And I'd like to think Live Nation realized, "Oh, these guys are talking about some stuff that is actually pretty fixable."

FIND COMMON GROUND

Based on the fixes that eventually emerged, there appears to be a lot to learn from the approach that Clyde and Jordan took when they met with the "opposition."

> CLYDE: I think that Jordan and I have probably an unhealthy amount of trust in people to be able to engage, that as long as what I'm saying is fair and reasonable, there's no way that you can get mad at me.

> JORDAN: It was really helpful for us that Live Nation [talks about being] "artists first." So we were able to say, "Oh, if you're 'artists first,' why are you not doing all of these things?" We're never trying to pull a fast one on anyone. We're never trying to stop anyone from making

a living. Ticketing is hard. The more that we dive into ticketing, there's a lot of complicated parts of ticketing that someone needs to be paid to handle. But are ticket fees insanely high right now, and is that unfair? Yes. So let's just try and balance this out a little bit more.

KNOW YOUR AUDIENCE

Long before they reached the negotiating table with Live Nation, Clyde and Jordan made sure they really knew what they knew, and what they didn't know. Here's Clyde again:

> We started engaging with venue reps as much as we could, almost comically, on certain things that we thought were so fucked up. And we would try this out on every venue rep. It would be like, "Yeah, so why is it that you deduct this number before this number?" And then sometimes we'd come away being like, "Wow, they actually had a pretty good reason! Much better than last night's guy." We tried to engage in the same friendly debates or challenges with every different industry person that we spoke to, to start to understand the reasoning, or what in large part turned out to be lack of good reasoning, as an underpinning for these things.

They entered these conversations in good faith, looking for information rather than just an argument. And like Christiana Figueres— the Paris Agreement leader who in Chapter Two explained why she solicits criticism from the Cassandras—Clyde and Jordan knew they ultimately would strengthen their own position by allowing the other side to punch holes in it.

CREATE NEW, BETTER NORMS

Having taken the lead on exposing questionable practices that other bands accepted as norms, Clyde and Jordan were ultimately invited to advise Live Nation on a program meant to loosen the grip that the touring industrial complex has on developing artists.

At its "club level" venues—such as the Fillmore in San Francisco, New York's Irving Plaza, Minneapolis's Uptown Theater, or Buckhead Theatre in Atlanta—Live Nation agreed to forgo its cut of the merch revenue, while also providing both the headliners and openers for each show with $1,500 in cash for gas and travel. The program, announced with no set end date, distributed tens of millions of dollars to more than four thousand artists in the first six months.[2] For a lot of musicians, those concessions can mean the difference between carrying on and packing it in.

It's notable that establishing new norms for the industry didn't require the muscle of a juggernaut band. To date, the musicians that have publicly taken on Ticketmaster or Live Nation have mainly been huge acts, like Pearl Jam or The Cure—groups with far wider renown than Lawrence. So, what made two guys from a band with a fraction of the fan base or experience level of those bands think they were up to the task? Clyde explains:

> Pearl Jam had a lot more hit records than we did, but I just have an ego about thinking that no one's going to be better than Jordan and me at having these arguments. We really know our shit and are good at debating. And, like, Jordan and I are so unintimidated by having a respectful and reasonable conversation with anyone, on whatever stage, at whatever level. And maybe that's what makes us

more well-suited to have this fight and win this fight than another artist—no disrespect to Pearl Jam.

Adam Grant, the Wharton psychologist who in Chapter Two discussed the importance of matching the right skills to the right roles, would probably say Clyde just nailed it. To that I would add one more observation. Working to make touring friendlier to artists fits right in with what Clyde told me his band's broader purpose is. "Our north star has always been, and will always be, making exactly the music that we want to make," he said. The cause he and Jordan were drawn to should help make it more affordable for Lawrence, and other up-and-coming bands like them, to keep doing just that.

LET THE MISSION LEAD THE WAY

The nice thing about operating with a mission that's more of an abiding concept than a concrete goal—like Lawrence's desire to create the music the band wants to make—is that it allows you to set benchmarks and invest deliberately in your future while still keeping you wide open to the unexpected opportunities that may come your way.

My brothers and I started AJR with a similarly simple mission, which also would prove quite stretchable: to engage audiences and keep them coming back. There are a number of reasons why I've always loved this goal:

It's timeless. The same aim applied when we were playing for audiences of twenty people and when we were playing arenas that seat twenty thousand.

It's achievable. We didn't have to wait to get to a certain size in order to meet the goal. If those twenty-person audiences in the early days were happy, then so were we.

It's measurable. We could easily track fan sentiment and ticket sales to ensure we were actually accomplishing what we set out to do—and if we ever found ourselves stalling or slipping, we could work on ways to fix that.

It's flexible. There's no one prescription for attaining this goal. We could get there by putting out music that connected with an audience, sure. But our tactics didn't have to be limited to that. That's why you've seen us employ so many of the fan base–building strategies covered in this book, like nurturing fan communities, designing fun games, lifting the hood on our production process, and putting on live shows we hope the audience won't soon forget. I suppose at times it may have looked disjointed from the outside, but everything was guided by the same overarching purpose.

Importantly, our goal wasn't beholden to specific behaviors or business models that easily could have become obsolete before we had a chance to accomplish what we wanted. This turned out to be essential in our industry, given how much change and tumult the music business has gone through just in the span of a decade or two. If our main mission at the outset had been to become the band with the biggest following on Tumblr, or to someday have the best-selling song on iTunes, it would have been a very short run.

Instead, our goal could be accomplished in myriad ways, with no defined ending point, no pressure to change platforms as the industry shape-shifted, and no need to move the goalposts as we grew. Best of all, there's an untold number and unspecified range of ways to keep fulfilling the mission for as long as we choose to, which leaves us open to all kinds of future opportunities, including ones we couldn't possibly foresee today.

FIGURING OUT WHAT'S NEXT

If your own long-term mission is feeling a little myopic now, don't worry. And don't stop working toward it! Even if it's not your forever goal, achieving a solid objective creates a terrific opportunity to start thinking about what else you can do.

NYC Pride, which you'll remember from Chapter Seven on live events, hasn't had to worry for years about making its centerpiece parade during Pride Month any bigger—the crowd of two million or more it attracts every June is already about as large as the city can handle. So it recently made a concerted effort to find other ways to grow. The organization discovered that there was a dearth of local programming for families with gay parents or kids, so it started hosting a series of family movie nights and an all-day NYC Youth Pride event with DJs and carnival games. Executive director Sue Doster has been thrilled with the response:

> Those have been crazy successful events. And that's because we kind of took a step back and looked at our constituency and said, "Are there areas that we aren't addressing that we could?" And I'm really proud of what we as an organization have done, because those events are really flourishing.

Sometimes when you reach a crossroads after checking off an important goal, what needs to be reevaluated are your own priorities. I recently had an interesting discussion about this with the comedian Jim Gaffigan, who was of course hilarious but also serious and a bit wistful when he spoke about it. Though he is neither a musician nor a movement leader, Jim has cultivated a huge fan base through a multifaceted career that he couldn't have possibly mapped out when he was getting his start in small comedy clubs in the 1990s. While he still performs stand-up, he has also written books, acted in movies, helmed a TV sitcom, co-starred in a Broadway play, and commentates regularly on the weekend news show *CBS Sunday Morning*. I wanted to know if Jim started his career with a specific goal in mind that, if he achieved it, would signal to him that he had truly succeeded. He did.

> For me, it was appearing on *The Late Show with David Letterman*. I had this idea that [if I did that] there would be a conveyor belt that would bring me into a room with Tom Hanks and . . . yeah, I don't know what I thought. Then I achieved that goal, which was very important to me. But, you know, I probably hadn't really been in what I would consider a serious relationship for five years; I probably hadn't had fun or connected with some of my friends for seven years. I had just been so focused. So I guess the point I'm making is, as you get to certain places, it makes you reevaluate.

His answer made me wonder what he attributed his success to. Was there a particular strategy or tactic that helped him reach his goal?

> I tried on a lot of different personalities [early on]. I mean, there was a time when I used to smoke onstage. But you end up going back to who you are. Honestly, it was when I was like, "Oh, all right, this isn't gonna happen" [that my career finally took off]. I had come to the conclusion that I'm grateful that I get to do what I love and I'm not going to necessarily make a great living at it, but I could probably exist in a tiny rent-controlled apartment in

downtown Manhattan, and that's what the universe is going to give me. Once the thirst disappears, you just can kind of focus on the craft, and focus on what you enjoy about it.

Postscript: Jim got married in 2003; he and his wife, Jeannie, have five kids; and the couple's experience as parents has become a staple of his comedy. Jim told me he thinks of his audience not as fans, but simply as "like-minded people." Had he not found his authentic voice or reevaluated his priorities after making it onto *Letterman,* other people "suffering from a condition known as children," as Jim hilariously described parenthood during our chat, would really be missing out.

This is probably a good time to point out that when you're crafting (or re-crafting) long-term goals or thinking through (or re-thinking) your plans for meeting them, sometimes it takes an outsider's eye to help you see all the possibilities. Ben Folds, who spoke with us in Chapter Seven about conversing with the collective effervescence in a live performance space, never imagined he would serve in the role of artistic director for the National Symphony Orchestra at the Kennedy Center in Washington, D.C., even though the veteran alt-rock musician had performed with hundreds of orchestras over the years. The idea of taking a position at the Kennedy Center was brought to Ben by his manager, Mike Kopp, a longtime political and corporate consultant who had never managed a musician until Ben came along. Working with someone from outside the music business may have cost him some more straightforward opportunities. But Ben, who has twenty-four years on me and has been playing music for a lot longer than I have, told me that as his career evolved, he specifically sought out a manager who would help him deviate from the industry's well-worn path.

I saw the horizon because it plays itself out over and over
again with sad, aging rock stars. I was turning down the
typical stuff because it didn't feel dignified. I wanted to do
something else. I didn't know what that was. . . . So I
opened myself up to a world of mystery opportunities by
signing up with Mike and cutting the cord with the other
stuff.

THE QUESTION I DREAD MOST

Thinking flexibly about the future is the surest path I know for
building anything in a sustainable manner, whether that's a band, a
fan base, a career, or a movement. And that's one reason why I absolutely hate it when I'm asked the question in the title of this chapter: *Where do you see yourself in ten years?* I'm often asked some
variation of this at the end of press interviews. While I appreciate
that I'm probably meant to answer in a way that leaves people on an
inspiring up note, I find the whole premise of the question annoy-
ingly misguided.

For starters, time is the wrong measurement for success when
you're talking about big goals. As a climate activist, I'd like to see us
reduce global carbon emissions to net zero. If we aim to get there by
2050 and the deadline passes, have we failed? Well, the planet will
have gotten warmer, and that will have lots of consequences for nature and humankind. But the project isn't over. We're still going to
be working toward the net zero goal, hopefully by pivoting to different, more impactful strategies. The timeline matters in that it may
affect the amount of collateral damage we suffer along the way. But
if a magic solution or a killer app or even just a really smart and
widely followed strategic plan materializes somewhere beyond the
bounds of our prescribed time horizon, and we use it to get our car-

bon emissions down to a level that can be fully absorbed by nature, haven't we still succeeded?

My even bigger problem with the "ten years" question is this: If you stay nimble, as I always aim to do, you gift yourself the sweet freedom to pivot in the future as needed, such as when there's a change in the conditions around you or a shift in your own priorities. Acting on this freedom can take you to (hopefully delightful) places you never expected. So yes, I can plan a year out, or maybe two, and I've certainly done so for concert tours and climate advocacy projects. But ten years?

A decade ago, I had no concrete evidence that AJR would make it as a touring band. I had no inkling I would earn a PhD. I had no idea I would someday start a nonprofit, grow my hair long, or write this book. So where do I see myself ten years from now? I have no clue! And I have absolutely no problem with that.

WHERE DO YOU SEE YOURSELF IN TEN YEARS, CHI OSSÉ?

> I hate this question so much. I mean, four years ago, I didn't
> know I was going to be running for office even two weeks
> prior to saying I was going to run for office.

New York City's first Gen-Z council member is apparently a kindred spirit. When I talked to Chi Ossé about his path into politics and advocacy (go back to Chapter One if you need a refresher), he was twenty-six years old and three years into his first term. The furthest he was looking ahead was to his 2025 reelection campaign. Otherwise, he sounded firmly focused on the present, which included a lot of work on affordable housing issues. He said he had recently helped bring more than a thousand people to a rent-guidelines board meeting (audiences for those are usually less than a dozen strong) to protest a proposal that would have allowed double-digit increases for "rent-stabilized" apartments, which are regulated by the local government.[3] A few months later, he celebrated a huge victory with the passage of his bill to shift the burden of brokerage fees from New York City renters to landlords. Affordable housing wasn't the issue that led him into politics—that was police funding, an issue that turned out to be even trickier than he thought to make headway on—but affordable housing is also an issue with great impact on his constituents. As Chi said:

> Maybe this is the politician in me now, that I've shaped up to be, but I have so much to deal with on the council. There are bills that I've put so much work into that need to pass. And I'm really trying to be present within this moment—because, one, I'm very lucky to be here and honored and appreciative of where I am; and also, I'm really happy. It's really fucking hard but it's something that makes me feel alive and brings some meaning to my life. But I think I can say, you know, in ten years I want whatever I'm doing to be meaningful, to be helpful to others . . . and [I want it] to be entertaining and cool. I don't know what that looks like. I don't know if that's within government or not.
>
>   . . . But I will always believe that the power lies with the people and that my job at hand is how to channel that power within a system that tries to diminish that power. And to relate that back to your question of what I want to do in the next ten years, I would love to grow that power, because I am reaching people who feel disillusioned, feel disengaged, and are probably uneducated about the power that they have, but that also exists within this de-

mocracy. So I want to see that grow, and I want to harness that, and I want to use it to continue to create the change that I set out to create the first day I went to a protest.

Okay. So maybe all those interviewers I've rolled my eyes at over the years actually knew something after all, because it turns out that the answer to the question of where you want to be in ten years really can leave an audience feeling inspired.

Speaking of, we're nearly at the end here. In an effort to end on an up note, I'd now like to ask *you* to project ten years out. Only I'm not going to ask where you see yourself in a decade. Chi's elegant handling of the question aside, I still don't think it's a particularly useful exercise for setting or measuring goals, which is what this last chapter is all about. Instead, I'm going to ask you to think about the future along somewhat different lines.

WHERE DO YOU SEE YOUR FANS IN TEN YEARS?

The whole reason I wanted to write this book was to give social change advocates a new toolbox for engaging people in their causes, inspired by the fan bases that have developed around artists in the music industry. True fans are passionate and community minded, and they're constructive critics when you need them to be. My hope is that with them at your side, the difficult work of social change will be spread across an ever wider and more deeply committed base of supporters intent on creating the progress we so desperately need.

At least some of that impact will hopefully be immediate. But these relationships might become even more valuable a decade or more into the future, as today's fans start taking on positions of greater political or societal influence. Jamie Drummond, the ONE Campaign co-founder we met in Chapter Eight, suspects this exact dynamic played heavily into Bono's early success as an advocate for foreign aid. Yes, there was also the U2 singer's commitment to carefully studying the issues, his ability to communicate both the prophetic and technocratic elements of a topic like debt relief, and what turned out to be a real talent at synthesizing different points of view and finding compromises. But before Bono could play the role of political strategist, he needed entry into the world's power corridors. I can confirm that this is somewhat easier for successful musicians than the average constituent. I've knocked on plenty of federal office building doors, typically to warm receptions. Many of the politicians and staffers I've met with have kids or nieces and nephews or young voters in their districts who are AJR fans, and I'm certain this has helped me to land an introductory meeting or two. But the political capital Bono held in the late 1990s was next-level. This was not only because he was one of the biggest rock stars in the world at that time, but because the powerful people he was meeting with were longtime fans.

U2, which had been making music since 1980, exploded globally five years later with a performance that *Rolling Stone* described as a "career-making moment" at the Live Aid concert for famine relief.[4] The internationally televised event, which if you remember from Chapter Seven had stages at Wembley Stadium in London and JFK Stadium in Philadelphia, was the Woodstock of its day. Only this time the message of peace and love was accompanied by urgent calls for globally minded activism. Tony Blair was thirty-two years old when Live Aid aired; Gene Sperling was twenty-five; Sheryl Sandberg was just shy of her sixteenth birthday. Why is this significant? Because a decade and a half later, when Bono started spending his social and political capital making global appeals for debt relief and a response to the AIDS crisis, Blair was the U.K.'s prime minister; Sperling was director of the National Economic Council under U.S.

president Bill Clinton; and Sandberg, who would later have a high-profile career in Silicon Valley, was chief of staff to the top official at the U.S. Treasury Department, advising him on things like the value of taking a meeting with a certain singer from Ireland. As Jamie noted, "The fans were running the world." And they were instrumental in helping Bono and his team create the change they wanted to see. Here's Jamie again:

> We can all say we have the power to change the world as young people, sure. And if we all listened properly and were sensible, we actually could change the world. But imagine if your fan base fifteen years later are still inspired by you and your music and your message, and they actually run countries or run the world's biggest institutions. You have a special kind of access then.

I genuinely love this thought. It immediately makes me wonder what messages we'll hear in a decade or two from the college students who grew up with AJR songs in their headphones, or what achievements we'll see someday from those little kids who wear trapper hats to our shows—no doubt they are going places. Gen-Z members of city councils might find ways to reorganize city budgets. Game designers might be able to create real social action through VR headsets. Gun-reform activists might see a year with zero gun deaths because of strict policies they develop. The people who can imagine the world they want to be rushing toward, and start rushing toward it now, have the potential to accomplish a lot of change in ten years.

The truth is, there is no time to waste. Protections for people and the planet are disappearing. But I do see glimmers of progress. In 2024, we played shows in seven states where fans were invited to take action on ballot measures defending the environment or human rights. Every single one of those measures passed.

Hope is not lost. It's not even deferred. It's just waiting for us to act on it.

So let's go.

Acknowledgments

My biggest thank-you goes to the number one "with" a boy could ask for. Without Heather Landy, there is no *Amplify*. From finding Graceland (figuratively) to jumping for joy (literally), this collaboration was endlessly educational, enjoyable, and emotional. I'd do it all over again anytime you're free. Thank you for taking a chance on me.

To Mila Rosenthal, my partner in thought and action, my courageous collaborator and my dear friend. Much of what this book fights for, I learned from you.

To my friends and family of all types who always say yes to my avalanche of ideas: Jack and Ryan, Shelby Kaufman, Xander Weinman, Steve Greenberg, Josh Russak, Mel Spiegel, Caleb Teicher, Liz Sears Smith, Doug Smith, Elise Stawarz, Jim Metzger, Ken Marvald, Cyndy Travis, Rob Marvald, Josh Marvald, Kelley DeMonte, Lori Spiegel, Larry Spiegel, Arjun Peruvemba, Nando, Samuel Levi Perman, Thomas Isen, Jonathan Birchall, Elektra Birchall, Isadora Ardizzoni, David Hogg, Fiona de Londras, Anya Schiffrin, Joe Stiglitz, Mary Robinson, Mark Berkowitz, Keith Albrizzi, Claudine Andrews, Jamie Young, Cole Tallerman, Jesse Tallerman, Suzanne DiBianca, Caryl Stern, David Gelles, the Peller Family, Ben Dahan, Katie Kavanaugh, Caleb Johnson, Li-Ya Mar, Zuleika Tesei, Veena Siddharth, Megan McLeod, Anh Vu Lieu, Jeff Opperman, Josh Kampel, Nadia Schreiber, Rebecca Kaplan, Hannah Needleman, Adam Gardner, Lara Seaver and the REVERB Team, Alex Edelman, and Benj Pasek, who helped me remember what my voice sounded like when I forgot how to speak.

To Allison Elbl and Alexa Price at Shore Fire Media.

To Jane von Mehren at Aevitas Creative Management, Matthew Benjamin and the team at Harmony/Penguin Random House, and all of the incredible people who contributed their time and words to this book. And to the fans—of course, the fans.

Most of all, thank you to Gary Metzger. You pushed me to find things that make me happy. I think I finally have.

Notes

CHAPTER 1: THAT THING YOU DO

1. Adam Met, host, *Planet Reimagined with Adam Met*, podcast, season 2, episode 1, "Accountability, Optimism, and Human Rights—Christiana Figueres and Mary Robinson," Planet Reimagined, September 16, 2021, https://open.spotify.com/episode/5KWYFwbwfqeBqMXWeW0JgV ?si=yvQvdM18SxKqu3nScM_h0Q.

2. Ibid.

3. "Wildfires," California Office of Environmental Health Hazard Assessment, August 23, 2023, https://oehha.ca.gov/climate-change/epic-2022/impacts -vegetation-and-wildlife/wildfires.

4. "Grand Rapids Rain Gardens Take Off in Popularity Following Demonstration Project," Michigan Department of Environment, Great Lakes, and Energy, June 21, 2022, https://www.michigan.gov/egle/newsroom /mi-environment/2022/06/21/grand-rapids-rain-gardens-take-off-in -popularity.

5. Nadja Popovich, Livia Albeck-Ripka, and Kendra Pierre-Louis, "The Trump Administration Rolled Back More Than 100 Environmental Rules. Here's the Full List," *The New York Times*, January 20, 2021, https://www .nytimes.com/interactive/2020/climate/trump-environment-rollbacks-list .html.

6. Jonah Engel Bromwich, "Combat Jack, Hip-Hop Lawyer Turned Podcast Pioneer, Dies at 53," *The New York Times*, Dec. 21, 2017, https://www .nytimes.com/2017/12/21/obituaries/combat-jack-dead-reggie-osse.html.

7. Calder McHugh, "A Party Promoter, an Activist and a City Councilman by 23, Chi Ossé Isn't Done Yet," *Politico*, August 8, 2022, https://www

.politico.com/news/magazine/2022/08/08/chi-osse-new-york-genz
-politician-00048183.

8. "District 36: Chi Ossé Biography," New York City Council, accessed
April 10, 2024, https://council.nyc.gov/chi-osse/.

CHAPTER 2: WHO ARE YOU?

1. Sam Stein, "Andrew Yang Ends His 2020 Presidential Bid," Daily Beast,
February 11, 2020, https://www.thedailybeast.com/andrew-yang-ends-his
-2020-presidential-bid.

2. "The Most Creative People in Business 2012," *Fast Company*, 2012, https://
www.fastcompany.com/most-creative-people/2012.

3. "Ranked-Choice Voting (RCV)," Ballotpedia, accessed December 15, 2023,
https://ballotpedia.org/Ranked-choice_voting_(RCV).

4. Jennica Lynn, "15 Things You Didn't Know About Bill Nye the Science
Guy," ScreenRant, March 5, 2017, https://screenrant.com/bill-nye-the
-science-guy-trivia-facts/.

5. Madeline Holcombe, "Megan Thee Stallion Wants You to Check on Your
Friends," CNN, September 27, 2023, https://www.cnn.com/2023/09/27
/health/megan-thee-stallion-mental-health-wellness/index.html.

6. Oliver Staley, "The Best Employees Are Not the Agreeable Ones, According to Adam Grant," Quartz, June 20, 2018, https://qz.com/work/1309735
/adam-grant-the-best-employees-are-not-the-agreeable-ones.

7. Thomas Grünhage and Martin Reuter, "Tell Me Who You Vote For, and
I'll Tell You Who You Are? The Associations of Political Orientation with
Personality and Prosocial Behavior and the Plausibility of Evolutionary
Approaches," *Frontiers in Psychology* 12 (May 18, 2021), https://doi.org
/10.3389/fpsyg.2021.656725.

8. Jesse Graham, Jonathan Haidt, and Brian A. Nosek, "Liberals and Conservatives Rely on Different Sets of Moral Foundations," *Journal of Personality and Social Psychology* 96, no. 5 (May 2009): 1039–40, https://doi.org
/10.1037/a0015141.

9. "Time 100: The Most Influential People of 2018," *TIME*, accessed April 27,
2024, https://time.com/collection/most-influential-people-2018/.

CHAPTER 3: WAXING LYRICAL

1. Annie Patterson and Peter Blood, "Cold Missouri Waters," Rise Up and
Sing, accessed March 11, 2024, https://www.riseupandsing.org/songs
/cold-missouri-waters.

2. Dan MacGuill, "Was 'Strange Fruit' Written by James Baldwin's High
School Teacher?" Snopes, April 28, 2021, https://www.snopes.com/fact
-check/strange-fruit-james-baldwin/.

3. United States Holocaust Memorial Museum, "Abel Meeropol: 'Bitter
Fruit,'" Jewish Perspectives on the Holocaust, accessed November 5, 2023,
https://perspectives.ushmm.org/item/abel-meeropol-bitter-fruit.

4. Ibid.

5. David Margolick, *Strange Fruit: Billie Holiday, Café Society, and an Early Cry for Civil Rights* (Running Press, 2000), 33–34.

6. Kat Eschner, "Billie Holiday's Label Wouldn't Touch 'Strange Fruit,'" *Smithsonian Magazine*, April 20, 2017, https://www.smithsonianmag.com /smart-news/billie-holidays-label-wouldnt-touch-strange-fruit-180962910/.

7. Aida Amoako, "Strange Fruit: The Most Shocking Song of All Time?" BBC News, April 17, 2019, https://www.bbc.com/culture/article/20190415 -strange-fruit-the-most-shocking-song-of-all-time.

8. David Pilgrim, "Strange Fruit," Jim Crow Museum, February 2008, https:// jimcrowmuseum.ferris.edu/question/2008/february.htm.

9. Amoako, "Strange Fruit."

10. "The Best of the Century," *TIME*, December 31, 1999, https://time.com /archive/6737430/the-best-of-the-century/.

11. Marc Eliot, *Death of a Rebel: A Biography of Phil Ochs* (Carol Publishing Group, 1995), 25.

12. Phil Ochs, "Here's to the State of Mississippi," Genius, accessed September 19, 2023, https://genius.com/Phil-ochs-heres-to-the-state-of -mississippi-lyrics.

13. Eliot, *Death of a Rebel,* 154.

14. Douglas O. Linder, "The Chicago Eight Conspiracy Trial: An Account," Famous Trials, accessed September 19, 2023, https://famous-trials.com /chicago8/1366-home.

15. Ibid., "Testimony of Philip David Ochs."

16. "Charting the Music of the War," *Modern Songs of War and Conflict,* from the Keesing Collection on Popular Music and Culture, Michelle Smith Performing Arts Library at the University of Maryland, accessed September 19, 2023, https://exhibitions.lib.umd.edu/songsofwar/vietnam/charting/home.

17. "The Nobel Prize in Literature 2016," NobelPrize.org, accessed September 19, 2023, https://www.nobelprize.org/prizes/literature/2016 /summary/.

18. Michael E. W. Varnum et al., "Why Are Song Lyrics Becoming Simpler? A Time Series Analysis of Lyrical Complexity in Six Decades of American Popular Music," *PLOS ONE* 16, no. 1 (January 13, 2021), https://doi.org /10.1371/journal.pone.0244576.

19. Ibid.

20. "Luminate Year-End Music Report," Luminate, 2023, https://luminatedata .com/reports/yearend-music-industry-report/.

21. Fred Moten and Hanif Abdurraqib, hosts, *Millennials Are Killing Capitalism,* podcast, "Building a Stairway to Get Us Closer to Something Beyond This Place," May 13, 2021, https://millennialsarekillingcapitalism.libsyn .com/hanif-abdurraqib-fred-moten-building-a-stairway-to-get-us-closer -to-something-beyond-this-place.

22. Ibid.

23. Ibid.

24. "Billboard Hot 100, Week of Aug. 27, 1988," Billboard, accessed April 11, 2024, https://www.billboard.com/charts/hot-100/1988-08-21/.

25. "Billboard Hot 100, Week of July 1, 2023," Billboard, accessed April 11, 2024, https://www.billboard.com/charts/hot-100/2023-07-01/.

26. "Lin-Manuel Miranda Performs at the White House Poetry Jam: (8 of 8)," Obama White House YouTube channel, November 2, 2009, https://www.youtube.com/watch?v=WNFf7nMIGnE.

27. Stephen Holden, "Putting the Hip-Hop in History as Founding Fathers Rap," *The New York Times*, January 12, 2012, https://www.nytimes.com/2012/01/13/arts/music/hamilton-mixtape-by-lin-manuel-miranda-at-allen-room.html.

28. "Old Man Stewart Shakes His Fist at White House Poetry Jams," *The Daily Show with Jon Stewart*, Comedy Central, 2009, https://www.cc.com/video/upaotm/the-daily-show-with-jon-stewart-old-man-stewart-shakes-his-fist-at-white-house-poetry-jams.

29. "President Barack Obama Chats with Jon Stewart about Hamilton the Musical While Backstage of The Daily Show!" *Hamilton* official Facebook account, July 26, 2015, https://www.facebook.com/HamiltonMusical/videos/president-barack-obama-chats-with-jon-stewart-about-hamilton-the-musical-while-b/1181735635186645/.

30. Gordon Cox, "Panic! At the Broadway Box Office: Brendon Urie Gives 'Kinky Boots' a Jolt," *Variety*, May 30, 2017, https://variety.com/2017/legit/news/brendon-urie-kinky-boots-broadway-sales-1202447897/.

31. "Yale Climate Opinion Maps 2023," Yale Program on Climate Change Communication, December 13, 2023, https://climatecommunication.yale.edu/visualizations-data/ycom-us/.

32. "Sandy Hook Promise Annual Report," Sandy Hook Promise, December 4, 2023, https://www.sandyhookpromise.org/who-we-are/financials/annual-report/.

33. David Riedman and Desmond O'Neill, "Shooting Incidents at K-12 Schools (Jan 1970-Jun 2022)," Naval Postgraduate School Center for Homeland Defense and Security, Homeland Security Digital Library (Monterey, California, n.d.), accessed October 22, 2023.

34. "Sandy Hook Promise Annual Report," Sandy Hook Promise, December 4, 2023, https://www.sandyhookpromise.org/who-we-are/financials/annual-report/.

35. "Public Service Announcements," Sandy Hook Promise, September 27, 2023, https://www.sandyhookpromise.org/psa/.

CHAPTER 4: LADDERS AND HURRICANES

1. Monique Mitchell Turner, "Harnessing Anger for Social Change," Research Outreach, June 3, 2020, https://researchoutreach.org/articles/harnessing-anger-social-change/.

2. kurt.rnc.edits, "World's Smallest Violin Anime Edit," TikTok, May 31, 2022, https://www.tiktok.com/@kurt.rnc.edits/video/71038802872427840 27?lang=en.

3. "Ice Bucket Challenge Dramatically Accelerated the Fight Against ALS," ALS Association, June 4, 2019, https://www.als.org/stories-news/ice -bucket-challenge-dramatically-accelerated-fight-against-als.

4. Alexandra Sifferlin, "Here's How the ALS Ice Bucket Challenge Actually Started," *TIME*, August 18, 2014, https://time.com/3136507/als-ice -bucket-challenge-started/.

5. Paul Clolery, "ALS Association Is Seeking More 'Wet' Donors," *The Non-Profit Times*, June 27, 2023, https://thenonprofittimes.com/donors/als -association-is-seeking-more-wet-donors/.

6. David Robson, "The '3.5% Rule': How a Small Minority Can Change the World," BBC News, May 13, 2019, https://www.bbc.com/future/article /20190513-it-only-takes-35-of-people-to-change-the-world.

7. Kyle R. Matthews, "Social Movements and the (Mis)use of Research: Extinction Rebellion and the 3.5% Rule," *Interface: A Journal For and About Social Movements* 12, no. 1: 591–615 (July 2020), https://www.interfacejournal .net/wp-content/uploads/2020/07/Interface-12-1-Matthews.pdf.

CHAPTER 5: HAMMERS AND STRINGS

1. "Synesthesia," Cleveland Clinic, accessed December 12, 2023, https:// my.clevelandclinic.org/health/symptoms/24995-synesthesia.

2. Heather Landy, "Pro Tools: Making Music Pop," Quartz Weekly Obsession newsletter, January 3, 2024, https://qz.com/emails/quartz-obsession /1851134835/pro-tools-making-music-pop.

3. AJR, "Breaking Down the Production of Weak and Birthday Party," YouTube, May 25, 2020, https://www.youtube.com/watch?v=x1A1 _QhGVHM.

4. Texas Civil Rights Project, "Texas Civil Rights Project Was Live," Facebook, June 17, 2018, https://www.facebook.com/TexasCivilRightsProject /videos/10155286391052035/.

5. Ginger Thompson, "Listen to Children Who've Just Been Separated from Their Parents at the Border," ProPublica, June 18, 2018, https://www .propublica.org/article/children-separated-from-parents-border-patrol -cbp-trump-immigration-policy.

6. Texas Civil Rights Project, "Live: Our Attorney Efrén Olivares Is Giving an Update . . . ," Facebook, June 22, 2018, https://www.facebook.com /TexasCivilRightsProject/videos/live-our-attorney-efr%C3%A9n-olivares -is-giving-an-update-outside-of-the-federal-cour/10155296801427035.

7. "Oficina Legal Del Pueblo Unido Inc./Texas Civil Rights Project IRS Form 990 for 2018," ProPublica Nonprofit Explorer, accessed December 22, 2023, https://projects.propublica.org/nonprofits/organizations/741995879 /201922819349300907/full.

CHAPTER 6: PRESS PLAY

1. Joyce Orlando, "Taylor Swift 'Breaks' Google: Swifties Looking for 'From the Vault' Answers Experience Glitches," *The Tennessean,* September 20, 2023, https://www.tennessean.com/story/entertainment/music/2023/09/20/taylor-swift-fans-vs-google-glitches-hit-hunt-from-the-vault-answers/70909689007/.

2. Ella Pulst, "Dema: Welcome to Trench," *The Dakota Planet,* February 17, 2022, https://thedakotaplanet.com/14559/features/dema-welcome-to-trench/.

3. Twenty One Pilots, "Twenty One Pilots—How Those Codes Were Solved (a Recap for Locals)," YouTube, June 24, 2020, https://www.youtube.com/watch?v=WI37JqBiYYs.

4. J. Clement, "Number of Video Game Users Worldwide from 2019 to 2029," Statista, June 18, 2024, https://www.statista.com/statistics/748044/number-video-gamers-world/.

5. Daniel Fernández Galeote et al., "Gamification for Climate Change Engagement: Review of Corpus and Future Agenda," *Environmental Research Letters* 16 063004, June 4, 2021, https://iopscience.iop.org/article/10.1088/1748-9326/abec05.

6. Taylor Swift, interview with Jimmy Fallon, *The Tonight Show Starring Jimmy Fallon,* video posted to YouTube by The Tonight Show Starring Jimmy Fallon: "Taylor Swift's Easter Eggs Have Gone Out of Control (Extended)," November 12, 2021, https://www.youtube.com/watch?v=hp3XS0q06Wk.

7. "Harvard Alcohol Project: Designated Driver," Harvard T.H. Chan School of Public Health Center for Health Communication, June 30, 2021, https://www.hsph.harvard.edu/chc/harvard-alcohol-project/.

8. Twenty One Pilots Wiki contributors, "Level of Concern/USB," Twenty One Pilots Wiki, accessed May 6, 2024, https://twentyonepilots.fandom.com/wiki/Level_of_Concern/USB.

9. Tyler Joseph, interview with Zane Lowe, "Twenty One Pilots, 'Trench,' Overcoming Insecurities, and What's Next," video posted to YouTube by Apple Music, September 5, 2018, https://www.youtube.com/watch?v=s4CLolgpHyQ.

10. Ibid.

11. "Yale Climate Opinion Maps 2023," Yale Program on Climate Change Communication, December 13, 2023, https://climatecommunication.yale.edu/visualizations-data/ycom-us/.

12. "Climate Expert Katharine Hayhoe: Help Solve Climate Change by Talking with Others About It," Hubert H. Humphrey School of Public Affairs, April 14, 2022, https://www.hhh.umn.edu/research-centers/center-science-technology-and-environmental-policy/advancing-climate-solutions-now/speaker-katharine-hayhoe.

CHAPTER 7: ALIVE NATION

1. University of Western Ontario, "Brain Waves Synchronize at Live Music Performances," Neuroscience News, April 9, 2018, https://neuroscience news.com/music-brain-synch-8740/.

2. Émile Durkheim, *The Elementary Forms of Religious Life*, translated by Carol Cosman (Oxford University Press, 2008, first published 2001 by Oxford), 175.

3. Kenneth Partridge, "Live Aid: The Complicated History of the World's Biggest Charity Concert," *Mental Floss*, July 3, 2022, https://www.mental floss.com/article/624770/live-aid-concert-history.

4. Peter Elman, "Tony Hollingsworth: Nelson Mandela 70th Birthday Tribute," Tribute Inspirations Limited, accessed on TonyHollingsworth.com, May 6, 2024, https://tonyhollingsworth.com/?q=content%2Fnelson -mandela-70th-birthday-tribute.

5. Charlie Hall, "Nelson Mandela: Iconic Images," *The Mirror*, July 18, 2012, https://www.mirror.co.uk/news/gallery/nelson-mandela-iconic-images -745769.

6. Nelson Mandela, "Address by Nelson Mandela at Wembley Stadium Concert, London," archived by the South African government, accessed May 6, 2024, http://www.mandela.gov.za/mandela_speeches/1990/900416 _wembley.htm.

7. Bob Allen, "2023 Mid-Year Business Analysis: Boxoffice Tallies Point to Banner Year," *Pollstar News*, June 26, 2023, https://news.pollstar.com /2023/06/26/2023-mid-year-business-analysis-strength-in-numbers-mid -year-boxoffice-tallies-point-to-banner-year/.

8. Bob Allen, "What a Friggin' Year! 2023 Boxoffice Results Remain at Record Highs,"*Pollstar News*, September 26, 2023, https://news.pollstar.com/2023 /09/26/what-a-friggin-year-2023-boxoffice-results-remain-at-record-highs/.

9. "Alameda Elementary Marks Two Years of 'Bus Bike' Exercise, Sustainability Ride," KATU News, April 24, 2024, https://katu.com/news/local /alameda-elementary-marks-two-years-of-bus-bike-exercise-sustainability -ride.

10. Émile Durkheim, *The Elementary Forms of the Religious Life*, translated by Joseph Ward Swain (Dover Publications, 2012; Project Gutenberg, November 13, 2012), 231, https://www.gutenberg.org/files/41360/41360 -h/41360-h.htm.

11. Ibid.

CHAPTER 8: GRACELAND

1. Glenn Beck (@glennbeck), "A total blast seeing @AJRBrothers at the @ToyotaMusicFac tonight. They are GREAT song writers, performers and lyricists. So fun and positive. I began to understand my son through their music years ago. SEE THEM if near you. THX AJR," Twitter, April 29, 2022, https://x.com/glennbeck/status/1519895572051804160.

2. Glenn Beck, "Biden Has Declared WAR on American Energy," Facebook, March 8, 2023, https://www.facebook.com/GlennBeck/videos/biden-has -declared-war-on-american-energy/239280091782346/.

3. Meredith Shiner, "Senate Torpedoes Background Check Deal," *Roll Call*, April 17, 2013, https://rollcall.com/2013/04/17/senate-torpedoes -background-check-deal/.

4. "Senators Commend Sandy Hook Promise for Successful Efforts Result- ing in 'Bipartisan Safer Communities Act,'" Sandy Hook Promise, July 11, 2022, https://www.sandyhookpromise.org/press-releases/senators -commend-sandy-hook-promise-for-successful-efforts-resulting-in -bipartisan-safer-communities-act/.

5. "Bipartisan Safer Communities Act of 2022," Ballotpedia, accessed March 22, 2024, https://ballotpedia.org/Bipartisan_Safer_Communities_Act_of _2022.

6. Bono, *Surrender: 40 Songs, One Story* (Alfred A. Knopf, 2022), 399–400.

7. Ibid., 357.

8. Nicholas Kristof, "When George W. Bush Was a Hero," *The New York Times*, April 8, 2023, https://www.nytimes.com/2023/04/08/opinion /aids-pepfar-bush.html.

9. David Gelles, "A Pop Star's Wonky Climate Campaign," *The New York Times*, March 12, 2024, https://www.nytimes.com/2024/03/12/climate /a-pop-stars-wonky-climate-campaign.html.

10. "What's the Deal with Methane?," UN Environment Programme, Octo- ber 18, 2022, https://www.unep.org/news-and-stories/video/whats-deal -methane.

11. Libby Nelson, "Glenn Beck Regrets 'Freaking Out About Barack Obama,'" Vox, November 7, 2016, https://www.vox.com/policy-and-politics/2016 /11/7/13556876/glenn-beck-obama-trump.

12. David Shere, "Sorry Glenn, We're Not 'Officially in Weimar Republic Territory,'" Media Matters for America, October 7, 2010, https://www .mediamatters.org/glenn-beck/sorry-glenn-were-not-officially-weimar -republic-territory.

CHAPTER 9: FEAT.

1. Steve Greenberg, "Steve's Best Songs of 2023: Plus an Essay!," S-Curve Records, January 17, 2024, https://s-curverecords.com/steves-best-songs -of-2023-plus-an-essay/.

2. "Billboard Hot 100 Songs Year-End Charts, 2023," Billboard, accessed May 1, 2024, https://www.billboard.com/charts/year-end/hot-100-songs/.

3. Ibid.

4. Daniel Hutchinson, "Catholics and Jim Crow, Review Essay," *The Journal of Southern Religion*, accessed May 4, 2024, https://jsr.fsu.edu/Volume12 /Catholics%20and%20Jim%20Crow%20Review%20Essay.html.

5. Robert Vamosi, "Anonymous Hackers Take On the Church of Scientology,"

CNET, January 24, 2008, https://web.archive.org/web/20120127212752
/http://news.cnet.com/8301-10789_3-9857666-57.html.

6. Esther Addley and Josh Halliday, "WikiLeaks Supporters Disrupt Visa
and Mastercard Sites in 'Operation Payback,'" *The Guardian*, December 8,
2010, https://www.theguardian.com/world/2010/dec/08/wikileaks-visa
-mastercard-operation-payback.

7. Misty Ring-Ramirez and Jennifer Earl, "Spillover Through Shared Agendas:
Understanding How Social Movements Set Agendas for One Another,"
Partecipazione e Conflitto: The Open Journal of Sociopolitical Studies, November 15, 2021, http://siba-ese.unisalento.it/index.php/paco/article/view
/24485/20315#.

8. "MAX," Spotify, accessed August 4, 2024, https://open.spotify.com/artist
/1bqxdqvUtPWZri43cKHac8.

9. Vivian H. Lyons et al., "Analysis of Daily Ambient Temperature and Fire-
arm Violence in 100 US Cities," JAMA Network Open, December 16, 2022,
https://jamanetwork.com/journals/jamanetworkopen/fullarticle/2799635.

10. Bim Adewunmi, "Band Aid 30: Clumsy, Patronising and Wrong in So Many
Ways," *The Guardian*, November 11, 2014, https://www.theguardian.com
/world/2014/nov/11/band-aid-30-patronising-bob-geldof-ebola-do-they
-know-its-christmas.

11. "Amplify: Building a Fan-Based Climate Movement," Planet Reimagined,
accessed August 4, 2024, https://www.planetreimagined.com/climate
-active-fellowship-23.

CHAPTER 10: "IF YOU WANNA ROCK, YOU GOTTA BREAK THE RULES"

1. *School of Rock*, IMDb, accessed January 3, 2024, https://www.imdb.com
/title/tt0332379/characters/nm0085312.

2. "Mandy—Jonas Brothers," Last.fm, accessed January 3, 2024, https://
www.last.fm/music/Jonas+Brothers/It%27s+About+Time/Mandy.

3. Billboard Staff, "Jonas Brothers Leave Disney's Hollywood Records," Billboard, May 1, 2012, https://www.billboard.com/music/music-news/jonas
-brothers-leave-disneys-hollywood-records-46397/.

4. David Kravets, "Dec. 7, 1999: RIAA Sues Napster," *WIRED*, December 7,
2009, https://www.wired.com/2009/12/1207riaa-sues-napster/.

5. Chuck D, "'Free' Music Can Free the Artist," *The New York Times*, April 29,
2000, https://www.nytimes.com/2000/04/29/opinion/free-music-can
-free-the-artist.html.

6. Andrew Dansby, "Metallica, Napster Settle," *Rolling Stone*, July 12, 2001,
https://www.rollingstone.com/music/music-news/metallica-napster
-settle-236089/.

7. "Education Department Approves $5.8 Billion Group Discharge to Cancel
All Remaining Loans for 560,000 Borrowers Who Attended Corinthian,"
U.S. Department of Education, June 1, 2022, https://www.ed.gov/news
/press-releases/education-department-approves-58-billion-group

-discharge-cancel-all-remaining-loans-560000-borrowers-who-attended
-corinthian-colleges.

8. "What They Are Saying: Leaders Praise Biden-Harris Administration Pause on Pending Decisions of Liquefied Natural Gas Exports," The White House, January 27, 2024, https://www.whitehouse.gov/briefing-room /statements-releases/2024/01/27/what-they-are-saying-leaders-praise -biden-harris-administration-pause-on-pending-decisions-of-liquefied -natural-gas-exports/.

9. "Annual Report 2022," Sierra Club, accessed March 22, 2024, https://static .sierraclub.org/foundation/annual-report/2022/.

10. "Our Finances," Environmental Defense Fund, accessed March 23, 2024, https://www.edf.org/finances.

CHAPTER 11: WHERE DO YOU SEE YOURSELF IN TEN YEARS?

1. Clyde Lawrence, "Taylor Swift's Live Nation Debacle Is Just the Beginning," The New York Times, December 10, 2022, https://www.nytimes.com /2022/12/10/opinion/taylor-swift-live-nation-clyde-lawrence.html.

2. "Live Nation's On the Road Again Has Supported 4,000+ Developing Artists & Will Continue Rolling Through 2024," Live Nation Entertainment, March 12, 2024, https://www.livenationentertainment.com/2024/03/live -nations-on-the-road-again-has-supported-4000-developing-artists-will -continue-rolling-through-2024/.

3. Katie Way, "Tenants Took Over the Rent Guidelines Board Hearing," Hell Gate, May 3, 2023, https://hellgatenyc.com/rent-guidelines-board -preliminary-vote-housing-activists-disrupt.

4. Gavin Edwards, "U2's 'Bad' Break: 12 Minutes at Live Aid That Made the Band's Career," Rolling Stone, July 10, 2014, https://www.rollingstone.com /feature/u2s-bad-break-12-minutes-at-live-aid-that-made-the-bands -career-242777/.

Index

ABOUT THE AUTHORS

Adam Met, PhD, is a musician, educator, and advocate. As the bassist in the multiplatinum band AJR, he has played for millions of fans worldwide. He is the co-founder of the climate research and advocacy nonprofit Planet Reimagined and teaches about climate campaigning and policy at Columbia University. He has contributed to numerous publications, including *Rolling Stone* and *Fortune;* has lectured at Aspen Ideas: Climate, EXPO, Chautauqua, and TEDx; and is a featured climate expert on CNN. In 2024, he received the TIME Earth Award and was named a *New York Times* Changemaker for his climate advocacy work.

Heather Landy is a senior editor at Bloomberg News and a former executive editor of Quartz. Her reporting has appeared in publications including *The Washington Post, The New York Times,* and the *Fort Worth Star-Telegram,* where she earned a Gerald Loeb Award for beat reporting.

ABOUT THE TYPE

This book was set in Fournier, a typeface named for Pierre-Simon
Fournier (1712–68), the youngest son of a French printing family.
He started out engraving woodblocks and large capitals, then
moved on to fonts of type. In 1736 he began his own foundry and
made several important contributions in the field of type design; he
is said to have cut 147 alphabets of his own creation. Fournier is
probably best remembered as the designer of St. Augustine Ordi-
naire, a face that served as the model for the Monotype Corpora-
tion's Fournier, which was released in 1925.

THIS MOVEMENT-BUILDING MANIFESTO INCLUDES
CUTTING-EDGE RESEARCH AND STRATEGIES FROM
TODAY'S MOST EFFECTIVE ORGANIZERS, ENGAGERS, AND
THINKERS, INCLUDING EXTENSIVE INTERVIEWS WITH

- **ADAM GRANT** (Wharton professor) on embracing disagreement within a movement

- **CHRISTIANA FIGUERES** (Paris Climate Agreement architect) on finding a path to solutions

- **ANDREW YANG** (former U.S. presidential candidate) on becoming the front person for your ideas

- **DAVID HOGG** (March for Our Lives co-founder) on the challenges of building a youth-led movement

- **CHI OSSE** (youngest-ever NYC council member) on working outside the box but within the system

- **SUE DOSTER** (NYC Pride co-chair) on keeping movements nimble and relevant

- **GLENN BECK** (conservative commentator) on finding common ground

- **JIM GAFFIGAN** (comedian) on setting and achieving goals

- **BILL NYE** (scientist and entertainer) on communication that connects with people

- **BEN FOLDS** (musician) on staying in sync with your audience

- **JAMIE DRUMMOND** (ONE Campaign co-founder) on the beauty of purposeful compromise

- **ENONGO LUMUMBA-KASONGO** (hip-hop scholar) on the intersection of activism and history

- **WENDY LAISTER** (Duran Duran manager) on harnessing the energy of live events

- **CLYDE LAWRENCE AND JORDAN COHEN** (of the band Lawrence) on pressing your argument

- **MAX** (musician) on the power of collaboration

- **SAM HOLLANDER** (songwriter) on aligning different perspectives

- **ASTRO TELLER** (co-founder of Alphabet's X division) on taking moonshots